EVERYONE'S ILLUSTRATED GUIDE TO TROUT ON A FLY

written by

R. Chris Halla

art by

Michael Streff

Frank Amato

PORTLAND

Published in 1996 by:
Frank Amato Publications, Inc.
PO Box 82112
Portland, Oregon 97282
(503) 653-8108

ISBN: 1-57188-098-4
UPC: 0-66066-00292-1

Printed in Canada

1 3 5 7 9 10 8 6 4 2

 # TABLE OF CONTENTS

HOW WE COME TO FISH FOR TROUT WITH A FLY

THE REASON EACH OF US FINDS OURSELF ON A TROUT STREAM CASTING A FLY VARIES. FOR ME, IT IS THE VISION IN MY MIND OF A SCENE FROM MY CHILDHOOD. IN THAT MENTAL PICTURE, MY DAD IS STANDING IN A SHALLOW, BUT FAST RIFFLE. THE WATER IS DOTTED WITH SO MANY SMALL ROCKS THAT WADING –EVEN STANDING– IS DIFFICULT.

A LONG LINE FLIES BACKWARD. ALMOST STRAIGHTENS, THEN COMES FORWARD AND DROPS. A SMALL DRY FLY ON THE SURFACE OF THE EMBARRASS RIVER. FROM OUT OF NOWHERE, A BEAUTIFUL SPOTTED FISH EXPLODES THE WATER'S SURFACE. THE FLY DISAPPEARS INTO THE MOUTH OF THE FISH.

DAD's ROD BENDS. THE FIGHT IS ON.

AND FOR ME, THE DREAM OF SOMEDAY BEING THE MAN IN THAT PICTURE IS BORN.

MANY PEOPLE COME TO FISH WITH A FLY BECAUSE IT WAS PART OF THEIR GROWING UP. SOME ARE JUST LOOKING TO EXPAND THEIR OPPORTUNITIES OR TO ENRICH THEIR FISHING EXPERIENCES.

SOME FOLKS WANT TO LEARN TO FLY FISH BECAUSE THEY READ A BOOK OR SAW A MOVIE, AND IT LOOKED LIKE FUN.

IT DOESN'T MATTER WHY YOU'VE DECIDED TO BECOME A FLYFISHER, A LITTLE HELP BEFOREHAND CAN DRAMATICALLY HEIGHTEN YOUR LEVEL OF ENJOYMENT.

WE HAVE TRIED TO INCLUDE IN THIS BOOK ALL THOSE THINGS YOU HAVE TO KNOW TO HAVE THE BEST EXPERIENCE YOU CAN FLY FISHING FOR TROUT. THERE ARE SO MANY OF THESE THINGS WE WISH SOMEONE WOULD HAVE TOLD US WHEN WE STARTED OUT.

R. CHRIS HALLA

MILESTONES

IN THE HISTORY of FLY FISHING

IN 1496, THE "TREATYSE OF FYSSHYNGE WYTH AN ANGLE" WAS PUBLISHED AS PART OF THE BOKE OF ST. ALBANS AT WESTMINSTER, ENGLAND. **DAME JULIANA BERNER** HAS LONG BEEN GIVEN AUTHOR'S CREDIT, BUT THERE IS LITTLE HISTORICAL EVIDENCE OF THIS.

THERE IS NO ABSOLUTE CERTAINTY WHEN AND **WHERE** FISHING BEGINS. BUT WE DO KNOW THAT FLY FISHING HAS BEEN EVOLVING FOR AT LEAST SIX CENTURIES, AND PROBABLY LONGER.

THE MOST FAMOUS FISHING BOOK OF ALL TIME, **THE COMPLEAT ANGLER**, WAS WRITTEN BY **IZAAK WALTON** AND PUBLISHED IN **1653**. FLY FISHING WASN'T MENTIONED.

FOR THE **1676** EDITION OF **THE COMPLEAT ANGLER**, WALTON ASKED HIS FRIEND **CHARLES COTTON** TO PEN A CHAPTER ON FLY FISHING. COTTON RESPONDED WITH THE CHAPTER TITLED "**HOW TO ANGLE FOR TROUT OR GRAYLING IN A CLEAR STREAM.**"

HISTORY OF FLY FISHING · CONT'D

IN **1870**, OR THEREABOUT, **HIRAM LEWIS LEONARD** BUILT HIMSELF A **FLYROD** THAT EVEN HE HAD NO CLUE WOULD MARK THE BEGINNING OF WHAT WOULD BECOME THE STANDARD OF AMERICAN CANE ROD BUILDING.

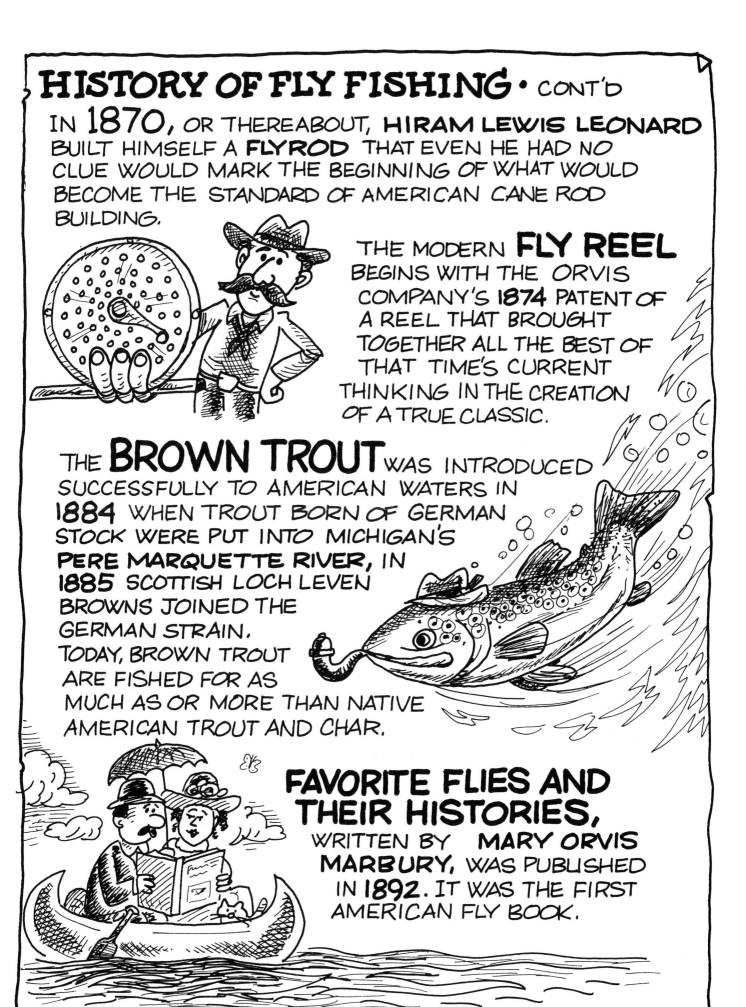

THE MODERN **FLY REEL** BEGINS WITH THE ORVIS COMPANY'S **1874** PATENT OF A REEL THAT BROUGHT TOGETHER ALL THE BEST OF THAT TIME'S CURRENT THINKING IN THE CREATION OF A TRUE CLASSIC.

THE **BROWN TROUT** WAS INTRODUCED SUCCESSFULLY TO AMERICAN WATERS IN **1884** WHEN TROUT BORN OF GERMAN STOCK WERE PUT INTO MICHIGAN'S **PERE MARQUETTE RIVER**, IN **1885** SCOTTISH LOCH LEVEN BROWNS JOINED THE GERMAN STRAIN. TODAY, BROWN TROUT ARE FISHED FOR AS MUCH AS OR MORE THAN NATIVE AMERICAN TROUT AND CHAR.

FAVORITE FLIES AND THEIR HISTORIES,

WRITTEN BY **MARY ORVIS MARBURY**, WAS PUBLISHED IN **1892**. IT WAS THE FIRST AMERICAN FLY BOOK.

HISTORY CONT'D

THE **CATSKILL** SCHOOL IS GENERALLY ACCEPTED AS THE BIRTHPLACE OF **AMERICAN FLY FISHING**. FROM THE **1840'S** TO AROUND **1920**, THE FLY FISHERS OF NEW YORK'S **CATSKILL MOUNTAINS** DEVELOPED THE **AMERICAN STYLE.** THIS IS, OF COURSE, NOT TO DOWNPLAY THE

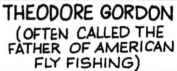
THEODORE GORDON (OFTEN CALLED THE FATHER OF AMERICAN FLY FISHING)

'QUILL GORDON'

CONTRIBUTIONS MADE TO FLY FISHING EVEN EARLIER ALONG THE REST OF THE EAST COAST.

RODERICK HAIG-BROWN, THE BEST KNOWN AND PERHAPS THE BEST OF WESTERN FISHING WRITERS, SAW HIS FIRST BOOK, **SILVER,** PUBLISHED IN **1931.**

EDWARD RINGWOOD HEWITT (1866-1957) WAS AN INNOVATOR AND A MASTER IN THE RANKS OF THE EASTERN FLY FISHING SCHOOL IN THE **1930s.** AMONG OTHER THINGS, HE DEVELOPED THE **BIVISIBLE,** ONE OF THE GREATEST DRY SEARCH PATTERNS, AND THE **HEWITT DAM,** AN INSTREAM STRUCTURE USED TO PROVIDE FISH COVER AND AERATE WATER.

'BROWN BIVISIBLE'

THE **FISHING VEST** WAS INVENTED BY **LEE WULFF** IN **1932.** LATER, WULFF WOULD BECOME KNOWN AS A LEADING CONSERVATIONIST AMONG ANGLERS AND, OF COURSE, AS THE ORIGINATOR OF THE WULFF PATTERN FLIES, INCLUDING EVERYONE'S FAVORITE FLY, THE **ROYAL WULFF.**

HISTORY CONT'D

IN 1936, **DAN BAILEY** TOOK THAT FIRST FLY FISHING TRIP TO MONTANA WHICH WOULD LEAD HIM TO CARRY THE EASTERN FLY FISHING STYLE AND IDEA WEST. THE MONUMENT TO HIS CONTRIBUTION IS A FLY SHOP STILL IN BUSINESS ALL THESE YEARS LATER.

PUBLICATION OF THE **STREAMSIDE GUIDE TO NATURALS AND THEIR IMITATIONS** IN 1947 SECURED THE PLACE OF **ART FLICK** IN FLY FISHING HISTORY. HIS BOOK IS STILL CONSIDERED A STANDARD REFERENCE.

THE FEDERATION OF FLY FISHERS was founded in Montana in **1965** to "conserve, restore and educate through fly fishing."

In **1959** a group of Michigan trout fishers met at the home of **GEORGE GRIFFITH** to form the organization that would become **TROUT UNLIMITED.**

THE HISTORY OF FLY FISHING CONTINUES TO BE MADE THROUGH INNOVATIVE COMPANIES AND INDIVIDUALS AND MODERN MASTERS SUCH AS LEFTY KREH, DAVE WHITLOCK, JOAN WULFF, NICK LYONS, GARY BORGER, DOUG SWISHER, A.K. BEST AND OTHERS.

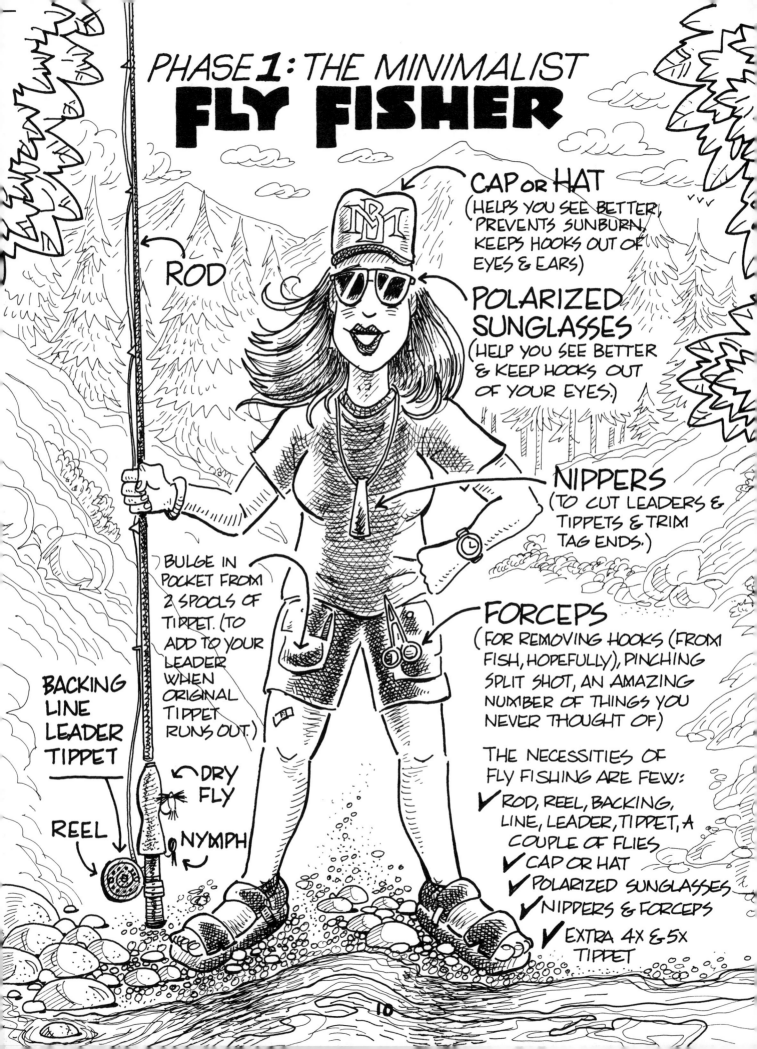

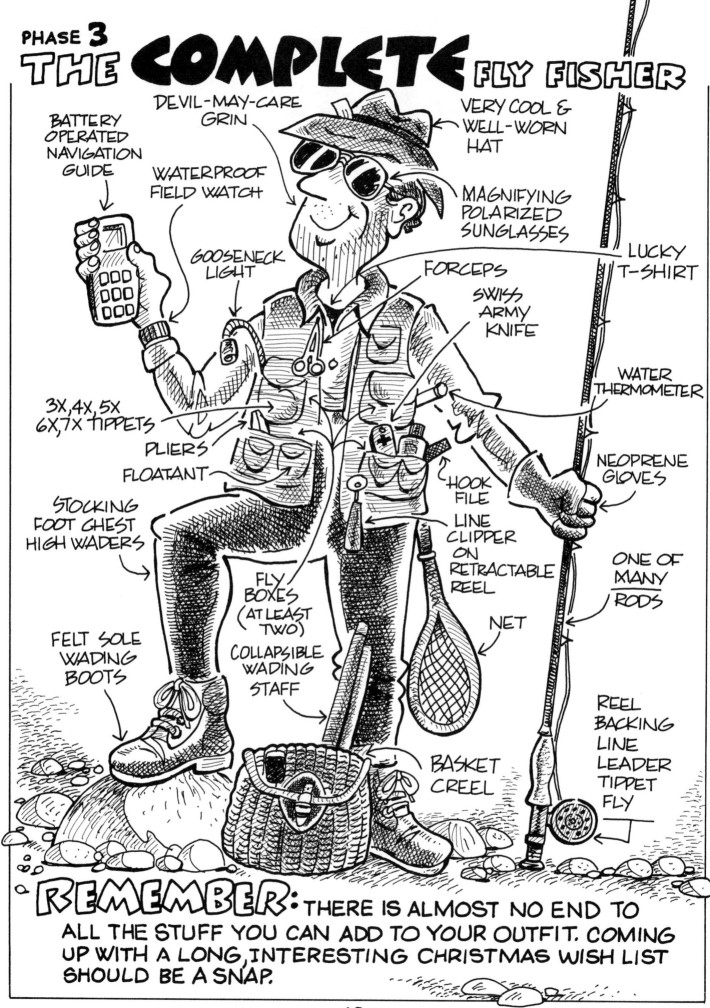

THE FLY ROD

THE FLY ROD IS THE APPARATUS BY WHICH THE FLY LINE IS CAST AND THENCE THE FLY IS DELIVERED TO ITS TARGET.

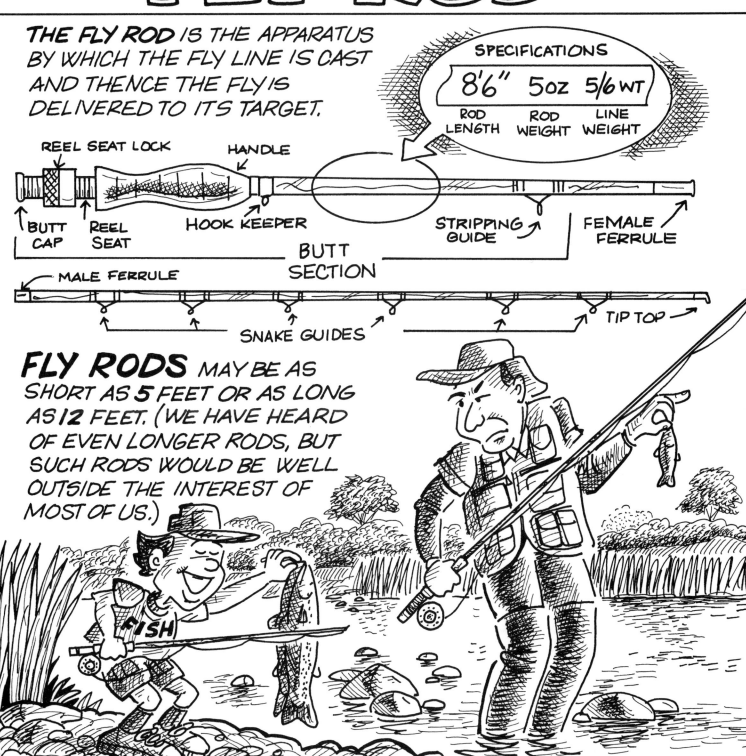

SPECIFICATIONS

8'6"	5oz	5/6 WT
ROD LENGTH	ROD WEIGHT	LINE WEIGHT

REEL SEAT LOCK

HANDLE

BUTT CAP

REEL SEAT

HOOK KEEPER

STRIPPING GUIDE

FEMALE FERRULE

BUTT SECTION

MALE FERRULE

SNAKE GUIDES

TIP TOP

FLY RODS MAY BE AS SHORT AS **5** FEET OR AS LONG AS **12** FEET. (WE HAVE HEARD OF EVEN LONGER RODS, BUT SUCH RODS WOULD BE WELL OUTSIDE THE INTEREST OF MOST OF US.)

FISH

THE MOST COMMON RODS RANGE FROM 6½ TO 9 ft., WITH 8½ ft. THE SINGLE MOST POPULAR LENGTH. YOU SHOULD CHOOSE YOUR ROD LENGTH DEPENDING ON HOW YOU PLAN TO USE IT.

IF YOU WILL FISH MAINLY **SMALL STREAMS** WITH LITTLE ROOM TO CAST, A **SHORTER ROD** SHOULD BE YOUR CHOICE.

FOLKS WHO WILL DO MOST OF THEIR FISHING ON **LARGE BODIES OF WATER** – SUCH AS LAKES – WHERE LONG CASTS ARE POSSIBLE, EVEN DESIRABLE, WOULD PREFER A **LONGER ROD.**

— FLY RODS ARE MADE OF **GRAPHITE, FIBERGLASS** OR **SPLIT BAMBOO.** GRAPHITE IS THE MOST POPULAR FOR A NUMBER OF REASONS HAVING TO DO WITH PRACTICALITY, EFFICIENCY AND COST. FINE BAMBOO RODS ARE VERY BEAUTIFUL AND VERY EXPENSIVE.

GRAPHITE

FIBERGLASS

SPLIT BAMBOO

MATERIALS & CONSTRUCTION WILL BOTH CAUSE **ROD** ACTION, OR FLEX, TO VARY.

THE *FLY ROD* CONT'D

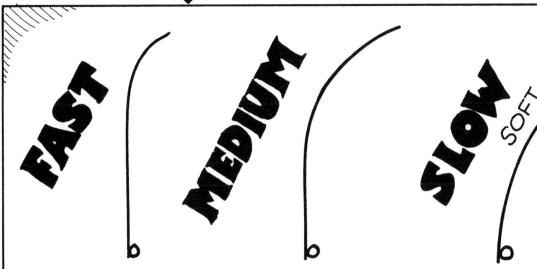

FAST **MEDIUM** **SLOW** SOFT

A FAST ACTION
ROD HAS THE SMALLEST DEGREE OF FLEX AND SNAPS BACK WHEN LOADED. (AT THE BACK OR FRONT OF THE CAST.)

A MEDIUM ACTION
ROD WILL FLEX FARTHER DOWN FROM THE TIP THAN THE ONE WITH FAST ACTION. THESE RODS UNLOAD (SPRING BACK) QUICKLY, BUT SMOOTHLY.

SLOW ACTION
RODS HAVE ALSO BEEN CALLED SOFT ACTION. THEY ARE FLEXIBLE TO THE POINT OF BEING WHIPPY. THEY LOAD & UNLOAD SLOWLY.

FUN FACT
EARLY ENGLISH FLY RODS WERE MADE OF WOOD (SUCH AS GREEN-HEART) AND WERE OFTEN 18 TO 20 FEET LONG!

WHILE CASTING IS THE FIRST CONCERN IN CHOOSING A ROD, ONE MUST KEEP IN MIND THAT A ROD'S OTHER PURPOSE RESTS IN ITS USE AS A FISH FIGHTING TOOL.

DON'T LAY YOUR ROD ON THE GROUND! WHEN FISHING IS DONE, TAKE IT APART AND PUT IT IN A ROD TUBE.

NOTE: BEFORE PURCHASING A ROD, TRY A NUMBER OF DIFFERENT TYPES. GET A GOOD FEEL FOR WHAT'S AVAILABLE. YOUR LOCAL FLY SHOP OR TACKLE DEALER SHOULD BE HAPPY TO HELP YOU PICK THE BEST ROD FOR YOU.

AT THE VERY LEAST, THE FLY REEL SERVES AS A STORAGE PLACE FOR THE FLY LINE. DURING CERTAIN CRUCIAL MOMENTS, HOWEVER, THE REEL SERVES AS THE BASE FROM WHICH FLY FISHING'S ULTIMATE BATTLES ARE FOUGHT.

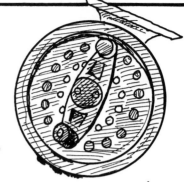

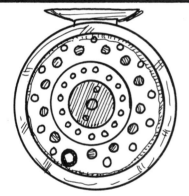

IT IS IN THE HEAT OF BATTLE THAT A REEL'S QUALITY BECOMES APPARENT. AT THAT TIME, THE ELEGANT MACHINE MUST ACCEPT STRESS, BRAKE & REVERSE QUICKLY, AND RUN OUT WITH JUST ENOUGH DRAG TO, EVENTUALLY, SUBDUE THE TROUT. AT ALL TIMES, THE REEL MUST PLACE THE ANGLER IN CONTROL OF THE **LINE**.

MOST REELS WILL EMPLOY EITHER **SPRING & PAWL DRAG** OR **DISC DRAG**. AT THEIR BEST, BOTH SERVE WELL THEIR PURPOSE OF ABBREVIATING THE FIGHT WITH THE FISH. ON SOME REELS, DRAG IS ADJUSTABLE. ON OTHERS, DRAG IS INCREASED OR DECREASED BY THE PRESSURE OF YOUR PALM ON THE RIM OF THE REEL.

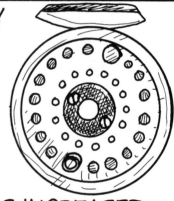

IT IS OF UTMOST IMPORTANCE THAT YOUR ROD AND REEL, ALONG WITH YOUR LINE, CREATE A *BALANCED SYSTEM.* IF YOUR ROD IS DESIGNED FOR FISHING **5** OR **6** WEIGHT **LINE**, THEN YOUR REEL SHOULD BE DESIGNED TO HOLD **5** OR **6** WEIGHT LINE. (AND, OF COURSE, YOUR LINE SHOULD BE EITHER **5** OR **6** WEIGHT TOO.)

NOTE: THE HOLES IN REELS REDUCE WEIGHT & HELP LINE DRY FASTER.

The FLY LINE

IT IS PRETTY MUCH AGREED THAT YOUR FLY LINE IS THE MOST IMPORTANT ELEMENT OF YOUR ASSEMBLED EQUIPMENT. **THE LINE IS THE SOUL OF THE SYSTEM.** (THIS BEING THE CASE, WE'LL TELL YOU RIGHT NOW THAT YOUR FIRST LINE SHOULD BE OF THE WEIGHT FORWARD FULL FLOATING VARIETY.)

8'6" for 7 wt line

SPECIFICATIONS PRINTED ON THE SIDE OF YOUR ROD TELL YOU WHAT WEIGHT LINE THE ROD IS BUILT TO HANDLE. YOU WILL CHOOSE A FLY REEL AND LOAD IT WITH FLY LINE APPROPRIATELY.

AFTER LEARNING TO FISH WITH A WEIGHT FORWARD FLOATING LINE, YOU MAY WANT TO TRY SOME OF THE OTHER FLOATING & SINKING LINES.

AFTMA

Fortunately, the American Fishing Tackle Manufacturers Association (AFTMA) has established a line standardization system that keeps us all speaking the same language.

Each line carries a **code** that tells you how the line is constructed, its weight & whether it floats, sinks or sits within the surface of the water (Intermediate Nuetral Density Line).

CONSTRUCTION/SHAPE

(THE FOLLOWING IS BUT A SAMPLE OF AVAILABLE LINE TYPES)

L LEVEL

DT DOUBLE TAPER — SAME TAPER ON BOTH ENDS

WF WEIGHT FORWARD — LONG, SLENDER FRONT TAPER

ST SHOOTING TAPER — 30' HEAD WITH FACTORY INSTALLED LOOP

WEIGHT (Based upon average weight of a grain of wheat)

LINE SIZE	WEIGHT	VARIANCE/TOLERANCE
1	60	54-66
2	80	74-86
3	100	94-106
4	120	114-126
5	140	134-146
6	160	152-168
7	185	177-193
8	210	202-218
9	240	230-250
10	280	270-290
11	330	318-342
12	380	368-392

TYPE **F** = FLOATING **S** = SINKING **I** = INTERMEDIATE

So, a WF5F line would be a Weight Forward, 5 weight, Floating Line.

NOTE: FLY LINE **BACKING** IS THE BRAIDED MATERIAL USED TO PREVENT YOUR FLY LINE FROM BEING TOO TIGHTLY PACKED ON THE REEL. IT ALSO GIVES YOU EXTRA INSURANCE IN THOSE EXHILARATING CASES WHEN A BIG FISH RUNS YOUR LINE OUT. ONE END OF THE BACKING IS ATTACHED TO THE REEL, THE OTHER END TO THE LINE.

THE LEADER & TIPPET

THE LEADER IS THE TAPERED, USUALLY MONOFILAMENT, CONNECTION BETWEEN THE FLY LINE AND THE FLY. (THE TIPPET IS, PROPERLY, THE FINE LEADING END OF THE LEADER.) A PROPERLY TAPERED LEADER ALLOWS THE FLY TO BE DELIVERED WITH ALMOST INVISIBLE SUBTLETY.

SOME FLY FISHERS INSIST ON BUILDING THEIR OWN LEADERS. MANY OF THE REST OF US ARE MORE THAN WILLING TO PAY THE PRICE FOR COMMERCIALLY AVAILABLE

KNOTLESS TAPERED LEADERS

EVEN THOSE OF US WHO CARRY FACTORY-MADE KNOTLESS TAPERED LEADERS ALSO CARRY SPOOLS OF EXTRA TIPPET MATERIAL TO REBUILD TIPPETS AS WE TIE ON FLY AFTER FLY DURING A DAY'S FISHING.

THE **LENGTH** OF LEADER NEEDED WILL BE DETERMINED BY HOW EASILY THE FISH WILL BE SPOOKED. ANY COMBINATION OF CLEAR, SHALLOW AND FLAT WATER WILL USUALLY CALL FOR A LONGER AND FINER LEADER. TYPICAL LEADER LENGTHS RANGE FROM

6 TO 15 FEET.

To BUILD YOUR OWN LEADER,

BEGIN BY DECIDING HOW LONG A LEADER YOU WILL NEED. (WHEN IN DOUBT, GO WITH **9 FEET** FOR DRY FLIES AND **7 FEET** FOR NYMPHS, WETS AND STREAMERS.

DIVIDE THE LENGTH OF THE LEADER IN INCHES BY **10**. THE BUTT END OF THE LEADER SHOULD BE ABOUT **30%** OF THE TOTAL, THE TAPERED CENTER ABOUT **40%** OF THE LEADER AND THE TIPPET ABOUT **30%** OF THE LEADER.

SAMPLE

$108 \div 10 = 10.8$ inches

$30\% = 32$ in. (approx.) $40\% = 44$ in. (approx.)

FOR THE **BUTT** END, USE MONOFILAMENT OF **20-25** POUND TEST, 0.18 - .020 IN DIAMETER.

THE TAPERED **CENTER SECTION** SHOULD BE MADE OF 4 EQUAL LENGTH PIECES NARROWING FROM .015 - .013 AT ONE END TO .008 - .007 AT THE OTHER.

THE TIPPET MAY BE 1 PIECE OR 2 DEPENDING ON HOW FINE A TIPPET YOU WANT AND PERSONAL PREFERENCE.

ON THE NEXT PAGE IS ONE SIMPLE FORMULA FOR BUILDING YOUR OWN LEADERS. THERE ARE A NUMBER OF OTHERS THAT ARE MORE COMPLEX AND POSSIBLY EVEN BETTER.

DID YOU KNOW?

FLY LEADERS WERE ONCE MADE OF SILKWORM GUT FROM THE SPANISH SILKWORM? THE GUT WAS BRITTLE WHEN DRY AND WOULD NOT STRETCH OUT ITS COILED MEMORY.

HERE'S A SAMPLE FORMULA (ONE OF MANY)

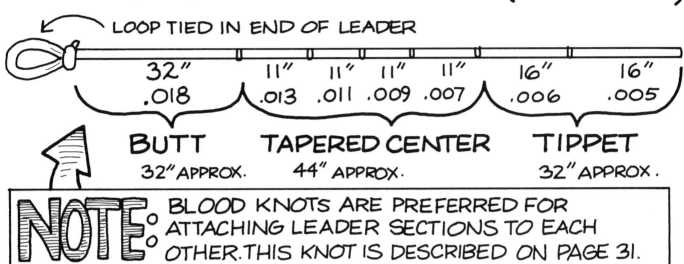

LOOP TIED IN END OF LEADER

| 32" | 11" | 11" | 11" | 11" | 16" | 16" |
| .018 | .013 | .011 | .009 | .007 | .006 | .005 |

BUTT 32" APPROX.   **TAPERED CENTER** 44" APPROX.   **TIPPET** 32" APPROX.

NOTE: BLOOD KNOTS ARE PREFERRED FOR ATTACHING LEADER SECTIONS TO EACH OTHER. THIS KNOT IS DESCRIBED ON PAGE 31.

TIPPET SIZE IS EXPRESSED IN AN **"X" NUMBER.** THE LARGER THE "X" NUMBER, THE FINER THE TIPPET. ALWAYS CARRY EXTRA SPOOLS OF TIPPET WITH YOU, WHETHER YOU BUILD YOUR OWN LEADERS OR BUY THEM FACTORY MADE.

X*	DIAMETER	SIZE FLY
0X	.011	2+
1X	.010	2-6
2X	.009	4-8
3X	.008	8-12
4X	.007	10-14
5X	.006	12-16
6X	.005	16-20
7X	.004	20-24
8X	.003	24-28

*Strength (pound test) varies by manufacturer.

WADERS
AND HIP BOOTS

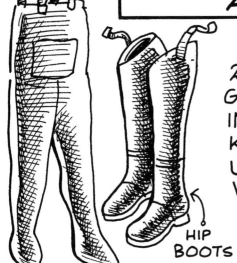

WADERS AND HIP BOOTS SERVE 2 PURPOSES: THEY KEEP US DRY - UNTIL WE GO OVER THE TOP OF THEM OR THE FIRST INEVITABLE LEAK APPEARS - AND THEY KEEP US WARM. AT LEAST THEY KEEP US WARMER THAN WE WOULD BE WITHOUT THEM.

HIP BOOTS

WADERS ARE MORE PRACTICAL THAN HIP BOOTS. THEIR HEIGHT ALLOWS YOU TO WADE DEEPER WITH GREATER COMFORT.

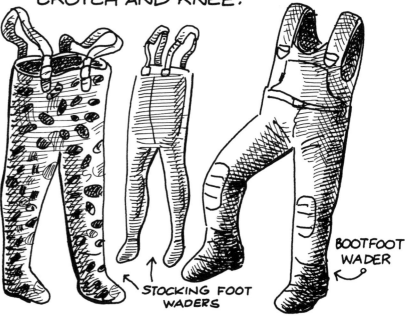

HIP BOOTS ARE SOMEWHAT MORE CONVENIENT, BUT THEY ONLY SERVE THEIR INTENDED PURPOSE TO A POINT ABOUT HALFWAY BETWEEN CROTCH AND KNEE.

WADERS AND HIP BOOTS COME IN A NUMBER OF MATERIALS AND STYLES. SOME ARE BETTER THAN OTHERS DEPENDING ON HOW THEY'RE USED, PRICES MAY VARY WIDELY.

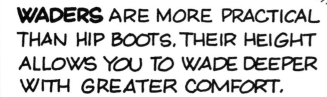

WADING BOOTS

STOCKING FOOT WADERS

BOOTFOOT WADER

NEOPRENE WADERS ARE GREAT IN VERY COLD WATER & FOR PEOPLE WHO GENERALLY HAVE TROUBLE STAYING WARM.

VESTS

THE FISHING VEST ALLOWS US TO CARRY ALL OF FISHING'S LITTLE NECESSITIES ASTREAM WITH US.

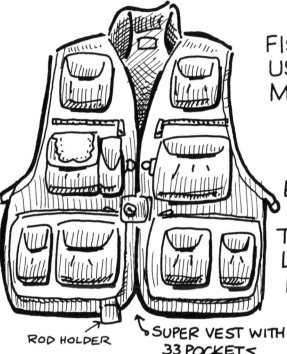

FISHING VESTS USUALLY HAVE MANY POCKETS INSIDE AND OUT, WITH ROOM FOR EVERYTHING FROM TACKLE TO LUNCH AND RAINGEAR.

ROD HOLDER

SUPER VEST WITH 33 POCKETS

COOL MESH VEST FOR WARM WEATHER

Vests come in a variety of styles and colors.

SHORT-STYLE VEST IS DESIGNED FOR DEEP WADING

PRE-VEST 'ERA FLY FISHER SETS OUT

The fishing vest was invented in the early 1930s by Lee Wulff.

OOPS!

SEVERAL STYLES OF INFLATABLE VESTS ARE AVAILABLE. SOME INFLATE ORALLY, WITH CO_2 CARTRIDGES OR BY BOTH METHODS.

MISCELLANEOUS NECESSITIES

THERE IS A SMALL SET OF ITEMS THAT, IF NOT FOR THEIR LEVEL OF IMPORTANCE, MIGHT OTHERWISE BE CONSIDERED MERE ACCESSORIES.

FORCEPS CONTRIBUTE GREATLY TO EFFICIENT HOOK REMOVAL. GET IN THE HABIT OF ALWAYS USING A FORCEPS OR ALTERNATIVE TOOL TO REMOVE HOOKS. THE FISH WILL BE MOST APPRECIATIVE.

ALSO GOOD FOR PINCHING DOWN SPLIT SHOT

NIPPERS, OR SNIPS, ARE USED MAINLY FOR CUTTING LINE, LEADER OR TIPPET. THEY'RE MUCH MORE EFFICIENT FOR THE PURPOSE THAN A KNIFE OR NAIL CLIPPERS. THE BEST NIPPERS HAVE A SMALL NEEDLE AT THE END FOR REMOVING KNOTS AND CLEARING GLUE-FILLED HOOK EYES.

SUNGLASSES

GOOD, POLARIZED SUNGLASSES SERVE THE DUAL PURPOSE OF HELPING YOU SEE THROUGH THE GLARE INTO THE WATER & KEEPING HOOKS OUT OF YOUR EYES.

PROTECT YOUR EYES AT ALL TIMES!

HAT

A HAT OR CAP IS A **MUST**, NOT AN OPTION. A FUNKY CHAPEAU MAY GIVE YOU JUST THE RIGHT LOOK, BUT IT WILL ALSO PROTECT YOUR NOGGIN FROM LONG DAYS UNDER THE HOT SUN, AND IT WILL HELP KEEP HOOKS OUT OF YOUR EARS.

NETS

NETS ARE DESIGNED TO MAKE IT EASIER TO LAND FISH. PROPER USE OF A NET LIMITS THE STRESS TO BOTH FISHER AND FISH.

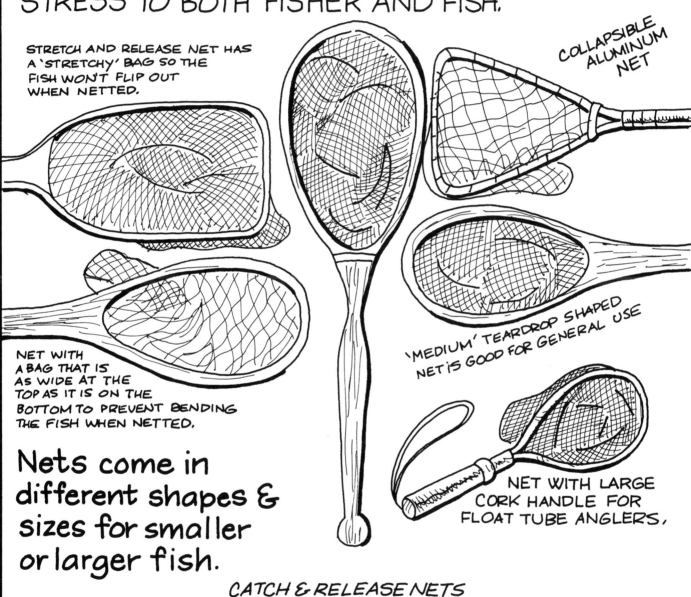

STRETCH AND RELEASE NET HAS A 'STRETCHY' BAG SO THE FISH WON'T FLIP OUT WHEN NETTED.

COLLAPSIBLE ALUMINUM NET

NET WITH A BAG THAT IS AS WIDE AT THE TOP AS IT IS ON THE BOTTOM TO PREVENT BENDING THE FISH WHEN NETTED.

'MEDIUM' TEARDROP SHAPED NET IS GOOD FOR GENERAL USE

Nets come in different shapes & sizes for smaller or larger fish.

NET WITH LARGE CORK HANDLE FOR FLOAT TUBE ANGLERS.

CATCH & RELEASE NETS

THERE ARE EVEN NETS WITH SHALLOW, SOFT MESH BASKETS, MADE ESPECIALLY FOR CATCH AND RELEASE FISHING.

25

ANGLERS AFLOAT

THERE ARE SOME GREAT TROUT WATERS THAT ARE JUST TOO BIG TO WADE. FORTUNATELY, THERE ARE A NUMBER OF WATERCRAFT THAT ARE -OR AT LEAST SEEM TO BE-DESIGNED SPECIFICALLY FOR FLY FISHERS.

FLOAT TUBES ARE PERFECT FOR MANY FISHING SITUATIONS. THEY ARE HOWEVER, AT THEIR BEST ON **STILL WATERS.** (RESERVOIRS, LAKES, ETC.)

USE A SHORT-HANDLED WADING STYLE OF NET.

NON SWIMMERS SHOULD <u>ALWAYS</u> WEAR A LIFE JACKET.

ANGLERS MUST WEAR FLIPPERS TO MOVE AND MANEUVER THE FLOAT TUBE.

ALERT: ANGLERS WHO TAKE FLOAT TUBES ONTO MOVING WATERS ARE AT RISK! IF THE FLOAT TUBE SHOULD FLIP, THE SAME DEVICE THAT HOLDS YOU AFLOAT OTHERWISE CAN TRAP YOU FACE DOWN IN THE WATER.

USE IN LAKES, PONDS AND MODERATE, SLOW-MOVING WATERS.

(USE OF A PERSONAL FLOATATION VEST IS RECOMMENDED)

Personal pontoon boats are excellent for many situations.

ANGLERS AFLOAT CONT'D

RAFTS have long been an excellent choice for fly fishing big, fast water.

The **McKENZIE BOATS** so popular on western rivers are the classic craft of fly fishing float trips.

These boats are easy to turn, hold steady in current and draw very little water.

27

Knots

There are many different types of knots used in the assembly of backing, line, leader, tippet and fly. Some are complex. Some are simple. Some fly fishers seem to know how to tie hundreds of knots. You really only have to know how to tie a few knots.

7 The 7 knots that follow here are basic to the arsenal of the fly fisher. They will serve you well. Learn them!

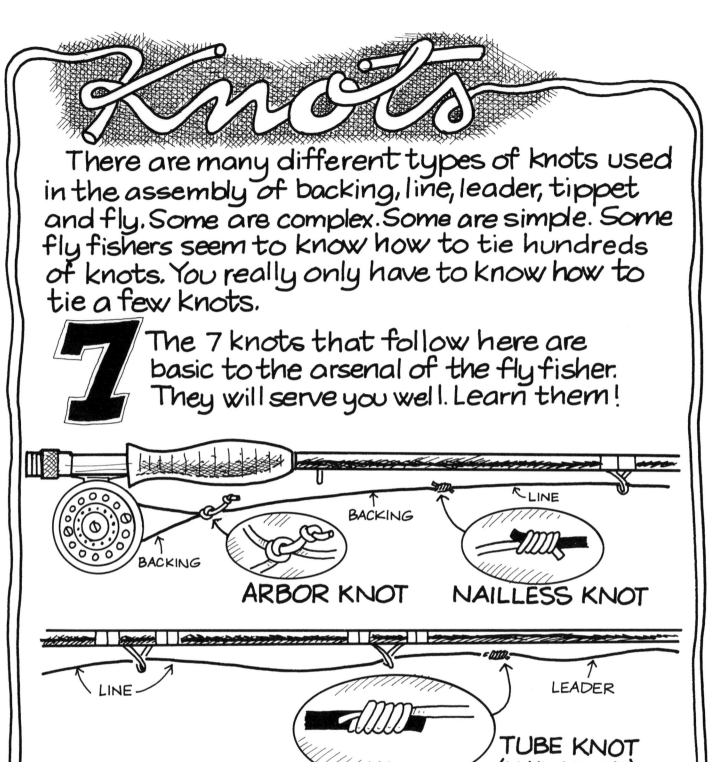

BACKING

LINE

BACKING

ARBOR KNOT

NAILLESS KNOT

LINE

LEADER

TUBE KNOT (NAIL KNOT)

LEADER

TIPPET

BLOOD KNOT

TURLE KNOT

→ **NOTE:** MOISTEN **ALL** KNOTS BEFORE TIGHTENING! ←

OVERHAND (ARBOR) KNOT

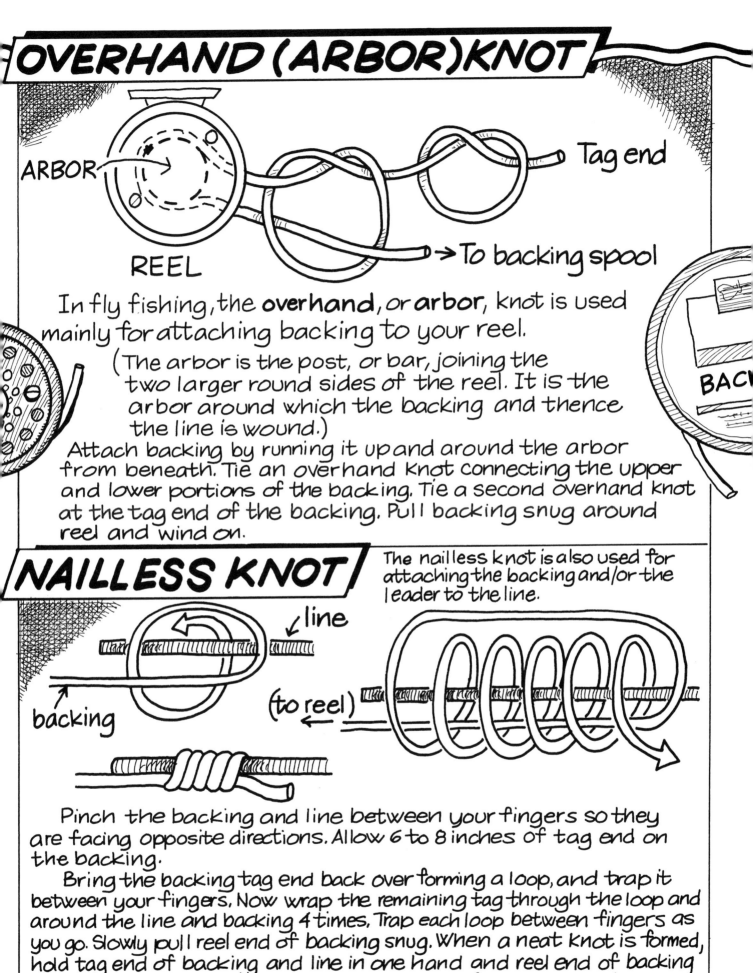

ARBOR

REEL

Tag end

→ To backing spool

In fly fishing, the **overhand**, or **arbor**, knot is used mainly for attaching backing to your reel.

(The arbor is the post, or bar, joining the two larger round sides of the reel. It is the arbor around which the backing and thence the line is wound.)

Attach backing by running it up and around the arbor from beneath. Tie an overhand knot connecting the upper and lower portions of the backing. Tie a second overhand knot at the tag end of the backing. Pull backing snug around reel and wind on.

BAC...

NAILLESS KNOT

The nailless knot is also used for attaching the backing and/or the leader to the line.

line

backing

(to reel)

Pinch the backing and line between your fingers so they are facing opposite directions. Allow 6 to 8 inches of tag end on the backing.

Bring the backing tag end back over forming a loop, and trap it between your fingers. Now wrap the remaining tag through the loop and around the line and backing 4 times. Trap each loop between fingers as you go. Slowly pull reel end of backing snug. When a neat knot is formed, hold tag end of backing and line in one hand and reel end of backing in other. Pull tight. Test by pulling on reel end of backing and line at the same time.

TUBE (NAIL) KNOT

The **tube** or **nail** knot is often used for attaching backing to line or line to leader. Whether attaching backing, or leader, the lighter material is tied onto the line.

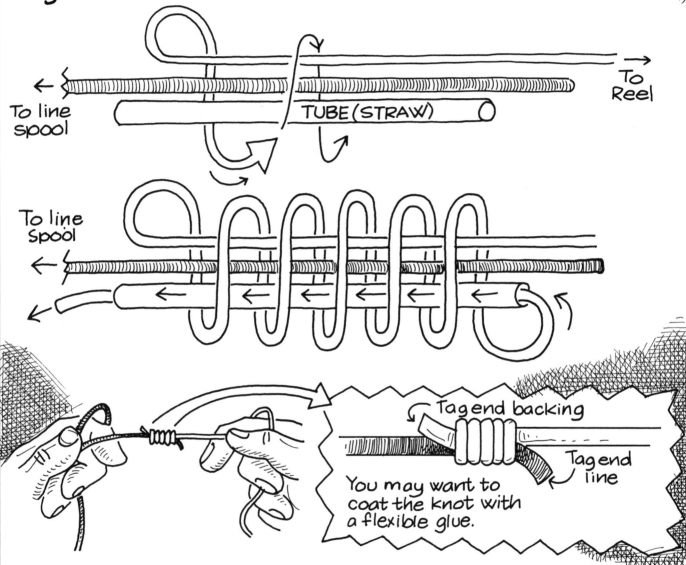

To tie the backing onto the line, hold a hollow tube or straw together with the fly line in one hand. Then lay in the backing, allowing for a 6 or 8 inch tag end, and hold it tight between your thumb and forefinger with the line and tube.

Make **5** wraps of backing back over the tube, the line and itself. As you wrap, pinch each wrap between your thumb and forefinger.

With wraps complete, run the backing through the tube. Carefully remove the tube. Pull both ends of backing tight. Finish by trimming tag ends.

BLOOD KNOT

The **blood knot** is used for joining leader to tippet or for "building" leaders. It will take you awhile to learn this one. But be patient, it's well worth the effort.

Lay the tag ends of the 2 "lines" you wish to connect across each other. Allow several inches of tag on both sides of the center.

Grasp the center of the "x" you have formed. Make **4 to 6** wraps with one tag end. Then loop it back and place it facing up in the middle of the "x."

Now wrap the other tag end around the same number of times. Bring it back and run it down through the center of the "x" that has now become an open, or somewhat misshapen, oval.

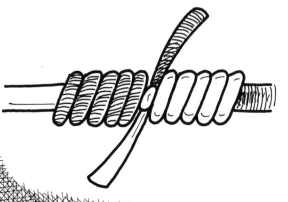

Finish by moistening and slowly, carefully drawing the knot together by pulling the standing ends.

The tag ends will be trapped, facing opposite directions, at the center of the knot.

The tag ends may be trimmed close without weakening the knot.

IMPROVED SURGEON'S KNOT

The improved surgeon's knot is a quick and easy way to join leader and tippet. It may be used instead of a blood knot.

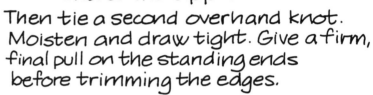

①

TO REEL ← LEADER → TO HOOK END

TIPPET

Lay the tippet against the leader, overlapping by several inches.

②

Loop around as though tying an overhand knot with the tag end of the leader and the standing end of the tippet.

Then tie a second overhand knot. Moisten and draw tight. Give a firm, final pull on the standing ends before trimming the edges.

③

④

UNIKNOT

The uniknot is one of the strongest you will find for tying on your fly!

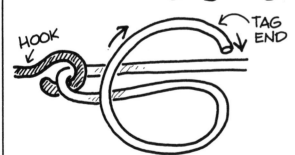

HOOK

TAG END

HOOK

TAG END

Pass the tippet through the eye of the fly (hook) and overlap by several inches.

Then loop the tag end back around and wrap the overlap 3 to 6 times.

HOOK

Moisten and hold the tag end while drawing the knot closed. The uniknot may either be slid down to the eye of the fly or left slightly above it to allow the fly freer movement in the water.

TURLE KNOT

The **turle knot** is an easy way to tie on a fly. The turle knot allows flies to swim naturally.

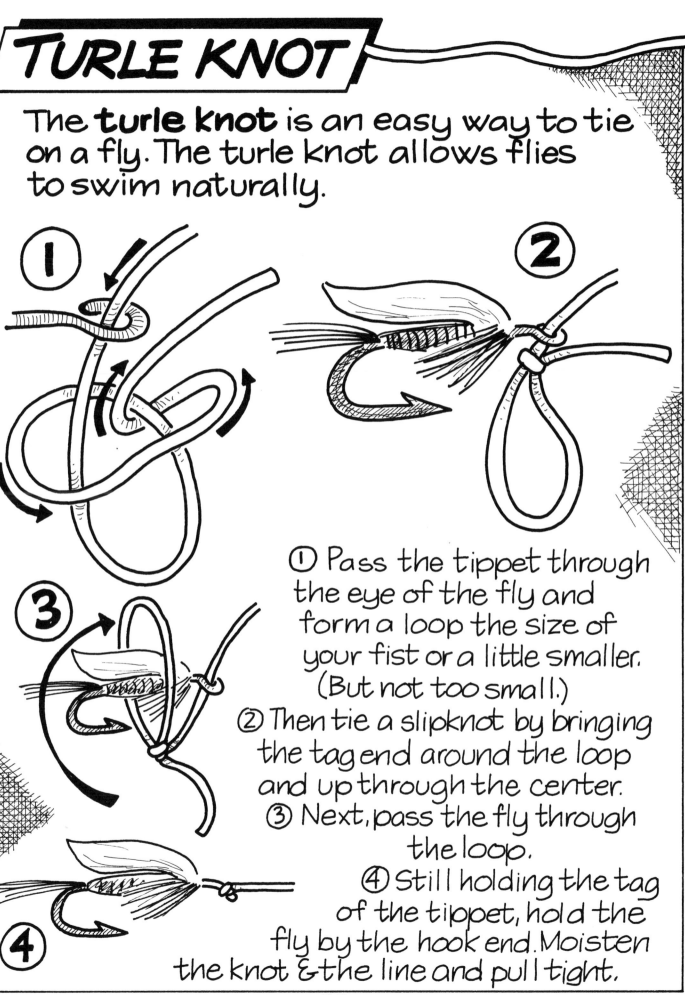

① Pass the tippet through the eye of the fly and form a loop the size of your fist or a little smaller. (But not too small.)

② Then tie a slipknot by bringing the tag end around the loop and up through the center.

③ Next, pass the fly through the loop.

④ Still holding the tag of the tippet, hold the fly by the hook end. Moisten the knot & the line and pull tight.

33

CASTING A FLY

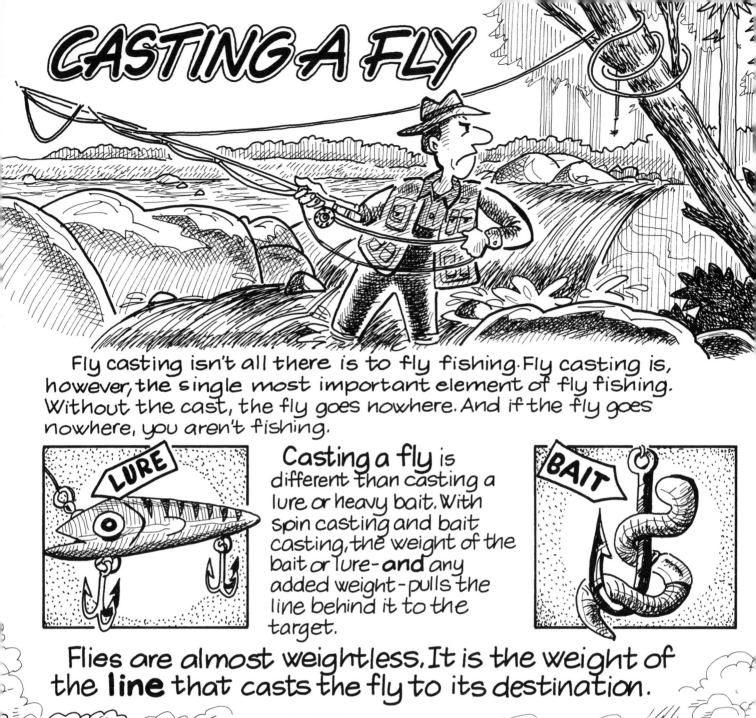

Fly casting isn't all there is to fly fishing. Fly casting is, however, the single most important element of fly fishing. Without the cast, the fly goes nowhere. And if the fly goes nowhere, you aren't fishing.

LURE

Casting a fly is different than casting a lure or heavy bait. With spin casting and bait casting, the weight of the bait or lure - **and** any added weight - pulls the line behind it to the target.

BAIT

Flies are almost weightless. It is the weight of the **line** that casts the fly to its destination.

MORE→

CASTING A FLY CONTINUED

Casting a fly is a complex thing. If you want to do it well, you must practice. (Fortunately, fish may be caught during the learning process.)

There are several basic casts you should learn right away. Master each one of them. Then learn to vary each according to conditions on the streams you fish.

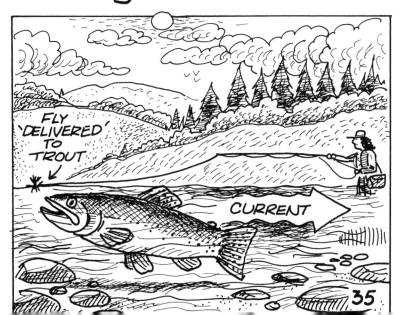

As you learn, concentrate on placing the fly upstream of the fish you're casting to. The trick is to do it without startling the fish with either the fly or the fly line.

PRACTICE! PRACTICE! PRACTICE!

BEGIN LEARNING TO CAST A FLY BY PRACTICING THE BASIC **PICK UP AND LAY DOWN** OR **OVERHEAD**, CAST. FOR YOUR FIRST PRACTICE SESSIONS, FORGET WATER. FIND A NICE, BIG OPEN SPOT IN YOUR YARD OR A PARK.

Yarn

Tippet

Dog

Lunch

20 to 25 feet of line

Lay your rod down on the grass, and measure out 20 to 25 feet of line from the tip of the rod. **DO NOT HAVE A FLY TIED ON AT THIS TIME!** (For practice sessions, tie on a piece of bright colored yarn.)

Now, pick up your rod. Good casting begins with a proper grip. Grasp the rod as though shaking hands with it. (With your casting hand, of course.)

Your thumb should be on top of the grip. Using this grip, the line will go in the direction your thumb points.

NOTE

For practice and when on the water, get in the habit of trapping your flyline under the middle finger of your casting hand.

PICK UP & LAY DOWN CAST

STAND WITH YOUR FEET ABOUT SHOULDER WIDTH APART. WHEN FISHING, YOU'LL USUALLY BE FACING YOUR TARGET DIRECTLY. FOR PRACTICE, TURN SLIGHTLY SO YOU'LL BE ABLE TO SEE BOTH THE FORWARD AND BACKWARD MOTION OF THE ROD AND LINE.

1 With your elbow at your side & bent at a 90° angle, your rod pointing in front of you.

Cock your wrist slightly.

2 Lift your forearm smoothly, bringing the rod straight up & back.

Keep your wrist cocked.

POWER STROKE 3 When the rod reaches just past 12 o'clock, stop moving your forearm.

Snap your wrist back.

4 Your line should form a nice tight loop in the air behind you.

Take a breath...

Nice loop!

5 As the loop opens and the line becomes nearly straight behind you (**DON'T RUSH IT**) begin your forward cast.

Don't rush!

POWER STROKE 6 ROD BENT

Push your forearm back in the direction you started and down to about a 45° angle (10 o'clock). **END** with a snap of the wrist in the direction of the target.

Lower the rod **slowly & smoothly** toward the surface of the water.

Line should drift down gently.

If the line splashes, either you have aimed too low or the forward cast was not delivered in one smooth action.

Loop Control

Good loop control results in good fly control. A nice **tight loop** is usually the key to a properly delivered fly.

Forward cast & back cast should be in line on a plane with each other

CASTING ARC

The LOOP is formed by the forward & backward motion of your arm & wrist. If the arc formed by your forward & back casts is small, your loop will be tight.

FORWARD cast & **BACK** cast should be in line with each other. And **do** concentrate on your **TIMING**.

Wide loops are air resistant, inefficient and difficult to control. Wide loops are caused by wide arcs.

Closed, or **tailing**, loops are air resistant and tie wind knots in your leader. They are caused by poor timing on the power stroke either forward or back.

38

FALSE CASTING

(FALSE BECAUSE THE FLY NEVER TOUCHES THE WATER)

Practice the pick up & lay down, or overhead, cast until you can pick up & lay down **30 feet** of line with ease. Then learn to **false cast**.

NOTICE THE NICE OPPOSING LOOPS OF THE FALSE CAST!

LIKE CANDY CANES!

To false cast you simply follow the same steps as with the pick up & lay down cast. EXCEPT, at the end of the forward stroke, instead of letting the line fall to the water, you repeat the back cast & so forth.

False casting is casting back and forth. False casting is **NOT** fishing.

When you're fishing, false cast only as much as it takes to let out the line you need or to dry your fly. In practice, however, false casting will help you learn line control.

CASTING ANGLE

A successful cast may be made at any angle from the water or your body as long as you maintain good loop control by casting in small arcs and keep your front and back casts on an even plane.

Practice casting from many different angles and you will be able to cast almost anywhere when others can't.

THE ROLL CAST

Sometimes there isn't room on the stream for a normal backcast. A **roll cast** allows you to fish many of these areas trouble-free.

Raise arm/elbow Slightly as you lift the rod back.

With your rod & line out in front, raise your forearm, bringing the rod & line back. Tilt the rod away from you slightly. Continue to bring the rod back until the line disappears from your line of sight (peripheral vision) to the side.

When you can no longer see the line to your side, bring your arm forward & down as though chopping.

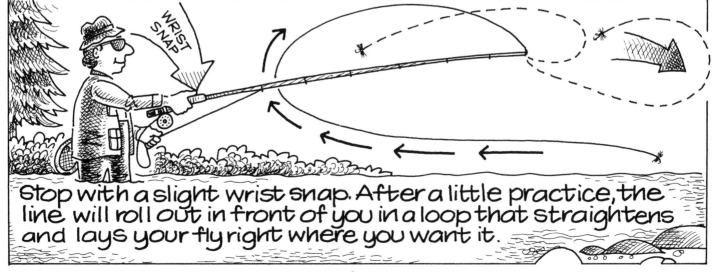

WRIST SNAP

Stop with a slight wrist snap. After a little practice, the line will roll out in front of you in a loop that straightens and lays your fly right where you want it.

SHOOTING LINE

Often you will want to cast more line than you have out in front of the rod tip. This can be accomplished easily by **shooting line**.

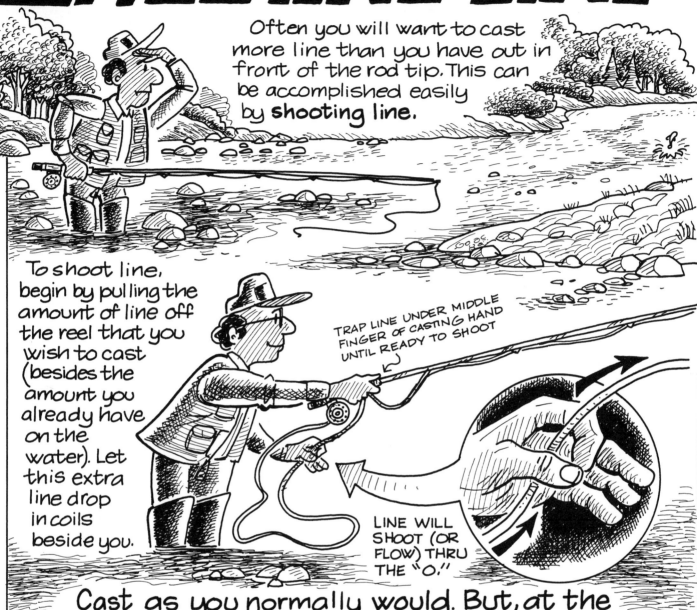

To shoot line, begin by pulling the amount of line off the reel that you wish to cast (besides the amount you already have on the water). Let this extra line drop in coils beside you.

TRAP LINE UNDER MIDDLE FINGER OF CASTING HAND UNTIL READY TO SHOOT

LINE WILL SHOOT (OR FLOW) THRU THE "O."

Cast as you normally would. But, at the end of your forward cast, just after the wrist snap, form an "o" shape with your thumb and forefinger, and release the line. The line will **shoot** through the "o" and lengthen your cast.

STOP

To brake or stop the cast when the line nears the target, close your fingers on the line.

THE STEEPLE CAST

With trees or canyon walls behind you, you can still execute a successful delivery of your fly by using the steeple cast.

To steeple cast, simply (but not quite as simply as it sounds) tilt your casting plane on an angle sharp enough to avoid the rearward obstruction.

DRAW BACK & UP, STOP AT 12 O'CLOCK ①

②

THE REACH CAST

Use a reach cast to make longer across-current, drag-free deliveries.

Make your cast as you normally would, except as your line shoots toward the target, reach upstream as far as possible with your casting arm. This maneuver keeps a "belly" from forming in your line as quickly as it would with a regular cast.

STOP THE LINE WHEN THE FLY IS OVER THE TARGET

THE WIGGLE CAST

One excellent technique for getting a longer drift downstream is the wiggle cast (aka "s" cast).

As your line shoots forward, wiggle the rod. At the end of the cast, lower the rod tip toward the water so the line lands in a series of "s" curves. To get an even longer drift, play out more line as the line in front of you straightens.

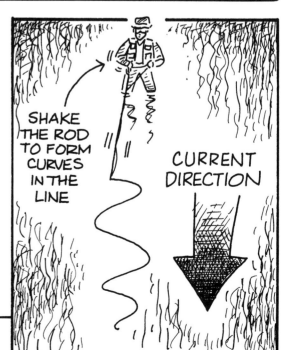

SHAKE THE ROD TO FORM CURVES IN THE LINE

CURRENT DIRECTION

MENDING & STRIPPING LINE

WHILE NOT TECHNICALLY PART OF CASTING, MENDING & STRIPPING ARE BOTH LINE CONTROL ACTIVITIES THAT CAN GREATLY ENHANCE THE EFFECTIVENESS OF EACH CAST. **MENDING** IS GENERALLY USED TO PREVENT DRAG, WHILE **STRIPPING** IS INTENDED TO KEEP THE LENGTH OF LINE AT PLAY MANAGEABLE.

A quick circular twist of the wrist 'flips' the line

CURRENT

MENDING can be done in a couple of ways. The first and easiest is to flip your rod tip in a semicircle, throwing the "belly" of your line upstream.

① UP TO 45°

② DOWN WITH A CHOPPING MOTION

CURRENT

You can also mend line by lifting your forearm to about a 45° angle then coming down with a chopping motion in an upstream direction. This action creates sort of a mini rollcast. Once perfected, it is a superior approach.

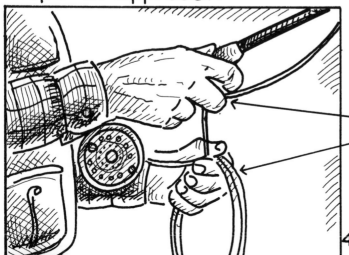

STRIPPING line is a basic skill essential to all fly fishing. To strip line, trap it under the middle finger of your rod hand, and retrieve it with your free hand. The only trick is to time your retrieve with the speed of the current.

TROUT FOOD

Trout eat a lot. And they eat often. Some fly fishers will only fish with imitations of adult aquatic insects. Others will only fish below-the-surface imitations.

If you want to have the greatest possible opportunity to catch trout, however, you will learn about all the foods they eat. Eventually your fly box will carry all sorts of aquatic and terrestrial life form imitations, so that you are ready for **anything!**

AQUATIC INSECTS

MAYFLIES, STONEFLIES, CADDISFLIES & MIDGES all excite the trout's palate during various stages in their lifecycles.

MAYFLIES are the most important aquatic insects to fly fishers, because there are so many different types available during each day and each part of the fishing year.

Trout will feed on mayfly nymphs below the surface, emergers as they leave their nymphal shucks in the surface film, adult duns as they dry their wings and fly away, and adult spinners as they drop back to the water's surface after mating.

DUN

SPENT SPINNER

EMERGER

NYMPH

PHEASANT TAIL

PHEASANT TAIL

GOLD RIBBED HARE'S EAR

STONEFLY

NYMPH

MONTANA STONE

MONTANA STONE

STONEFLIES aren't as readily available as other aquatic insects, but on the streams where they are found, the trout feed with gusto. Stoneflies are available to the fish both as nymphs and as adults when they return to the water's surface to lay eggs.

TED'S STONE

TED'S STONE

AQUATIC INSECTS CONT'D

CADDISFLIES are common and come in great variety. (There are hundreds of species!) Where there is water, there are usually *some* caddisflies. Trout take caddisflies as larvae, pupae and adults.

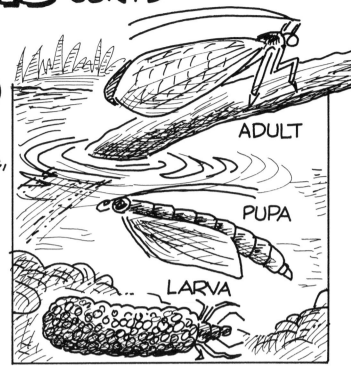

ADULT

PUPA

LARVA

HENRYVILLE SPECIAL

ELK HAIR CADDIS

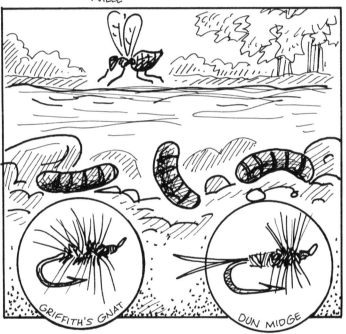

GRIFFITH'S GNAT

DUN MIDGE

MIDGES are such tiny bugs that many flyfishers ignore them completely. Trout, on the other hand, are very aware of the existence of midges and, at times, will feed on them with abandon. Most midges are taken by trout as pupae in the surface film, though some are taken as escaping adults.

OTHER AQUATIC LIFE FORMS

Minnows and crayfish, leeches and worms, scuds (fresh-water shrimp), even snails make up part of a trout's diet.

WORM

SCUD

MINNOW

CRAYFISH

SNAIL

TERRESTRIALS

TERRESTRIALS are trout favorites when they're available. Ants, grasshoppers & beetles often fall into the water & get slurped up by opportunistic trout. Even bees have been seen to disappear in a frenzied rise.

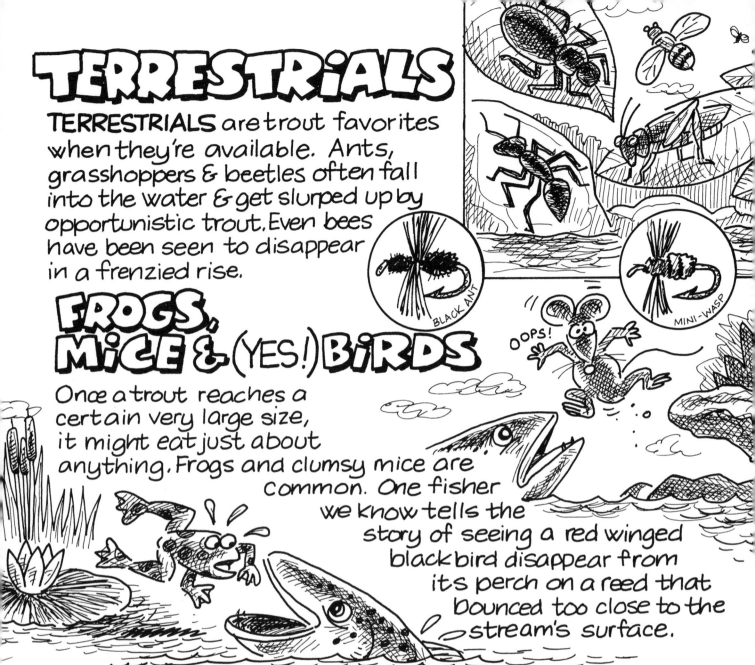

BLACK ANT

MINI-WASP

OOPS!

FROGS, MICE & (YES!) BIRDS

Once a trout reaches a certain very large size, it might eat just about anything. Frogs and clumsy mice are common. One fisher we know tells the story of seeing a red winged blackbird disappear from its perch on a reed that bounced too close to the stream's surface.

HOW TO FOOL A TROUT WITH FAKE FOOD

THERE ARE POSSIBLY 1,000s OF FLIES TIED TO IMITATE THE THINGS TROUT EAT. EACH REGION WILL HAVE ITS OWN FAVORITE FLIES. ALWAYS STOP IN AT LOCAL FLY SHOPS TO FIND OUT WHAT THE CURRENT HOT NUMBER IS, BUT ALWAYS CARRY A BASIC SELECTION OF FLIES WITH SOME PROMISE OF WORKING ALMOST ANYWHERE. ON THE FOLLOWING PAGES, WE RECOMMEND WHAT WE THINK ARE SOME OF THE ESSENTIAL FLIES. WE'VE ALSO INCLUDED THE DRESSING, OR RECIPE, FOR EACH OF OUR ESSENTIAL FLIES SO YOU HAVE AN IDEA WHAT FLIES ARE MADE OF.

ADAMS

HOOK · Dry fly   SIZES · 14·16·18·20
THREAD · Black
TAIL · Mixed grizzly & brown hackle barbules
BODY · Dubbed gray muskrat
WINGS · Grizzly hackle tips
HACKLE · One grizzly & one brown

BLACK GNAT

HOOK · Dry Fly   SIZES · 14·16·18·20
THREAD · Black
TAIL · Black hackle barbules
BODY · Dubbed black dyed beaver or muskrat
WINGS · Gray mallard wing quill sections
HACKLE · Two black hackles

BLUE-WINGED OLIVE

HOOK · Dry Fly   SIZES · 16·18·20·22
THREAD · Olive
TAIL · Blue dun hackle barbules
BODY · Dubbed olive beaver
WINGS · Dark blue dun hackle tips
HACKLE · Blue dun

ELK HAIR CADDIS

HOOK · Dry fly   SIZES · 12·14·16·18
THREAD · Tan
BODY · Light yellow or light green
HACKLE · One palmered grizzly hackle
WING · Elk body hair

ROYAL WULFF

HOOK · Dry fly   SIZES · 10·12·14·16
THREAD · Black
TAIL · Brown hackle barbules
BODY · Peacock
WINGS · White calftail
HACKLE · Two brown hackles

ESSENTIAL NYMPHS ETC

GOLD RIBBED HARE'S EAR

HOOK · Nymph SIZES · 10·12·14·16
THREAD · Brown
TAIL · Hare's mask fibers
ABDOMEN · Fine hare's ear
RIBBING · Fine flat gold tinsel
WINGCASE · Turkey wing quill section
THORAX · Coarse hare's ear

MARCH BROWN

HOOK · Nymph SIZES · 10·12·14·16
THREAD · Orange
TAIL · Ringneck pheasant tail feather barbules
BODY · Dubbed red fox fur
WINGCASE · Mallard flank
HACKLE · One palmered brown hackle
THORAX · Dubbed red fox

PHEASANT TAIL NYMPH

HOOK · Nymph SIZES · 10·12·14·16
THREAD · Brown
TAIL · Ringneck pheasant tail barbules
ABDOMEN · Pheasant tail barbules
RIB · Medium-fine copper wire
WINGCASE · Pheasant tail barbules
THORAX · Dubbed brown possum

PRINCE NYMPH

HOOK · Nymph SIZES · 10·12·14·16
THREAD · Black
TAIL · Brown goose biots
BODY · Peacock herl
WING · Two white goose biots
HACKLE · Soft brown hackle

OLIVE SCUD

HOOK · Nymph or scud
SIZES · 10·12·14·16
THREAD · Olive
TAIL · Krystal flash & olive thread
BODY · Dubbed olive dyed rabbit
OVERBODY · Clear elastic
RIBBING · Fine copper wire

ESSENTIAL STREAMERS

MICKEY FINN

MUDDLER MINNOW

HOOK · Streamer **SIZES** · 6 · 8 · 10 · 12
THREAD · Black
BODY · Flat silver tinsel
RIB · Oval silver tinsel
WING · Yellow bucktail, red bucktail, yellow bucktail

HOOK · Streamer or 2x dry fly
SIZES · 1/0 · 2 · 4 · 6 · 10 · 12
THREAD · Black
TAIL · Mottled turkey quill
BODY · Gold tinsel
UNDERWING · Gray squirrel
OVERWING · Pair mottled turkey wings
HEAD · Spun deer body hair

ESSENTIAL TERRESTRIALS

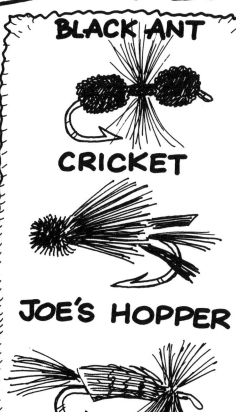

BLACK ANT

CRICKET

JOE'S HOPPER

HOOK · Dry fly
SIZES · 14 · 16 · 18 · 20
THREAD · Black
ABDOMEN · Dubbed black dyed beaver
HACKLE · Sparse black hackle tied between body sections

HOOK · Dry fly **SIZES** · 8 · 10 · 12 · 14
THREAD · Black
ABDOMEN · Dubbed dark brown Possum
WING · Dark or dyed black turkey wing sections
HEAD · Spun black deer hair

HOOK · Dry fly **SIZES** · 6 · 8 · 10 · 12
THREAD · Brown
TAIL · Brown hackle barbules
BODY · Yellow chenille
RIB · Palmered brown hackle
WING · Mottled turkey wing sections
HACKLE · One brown & one grizzly hackle

Reading Water

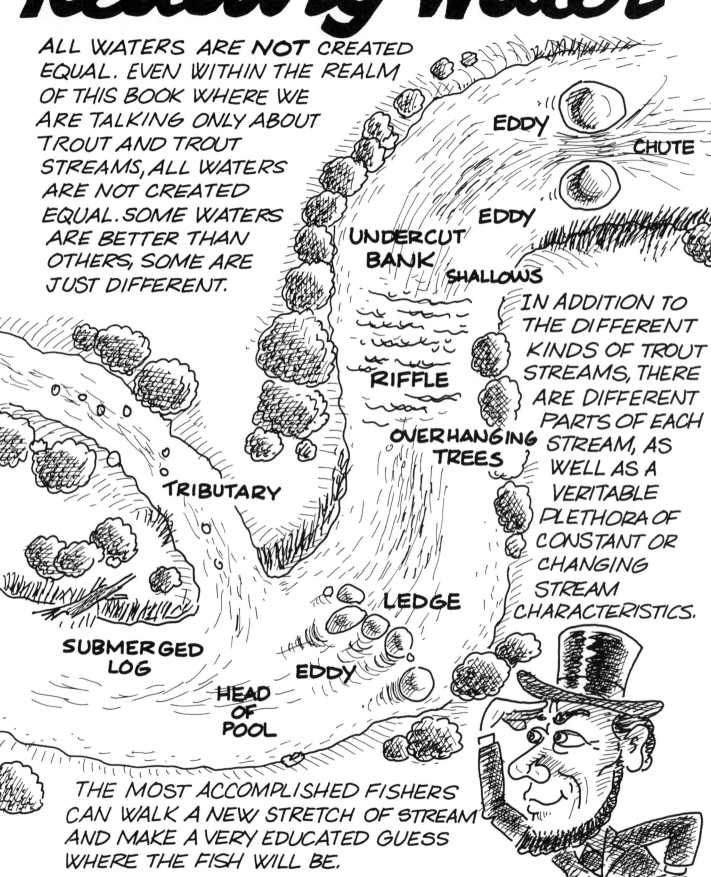

ALL WATERS ARE **NOT** CREATED EQUAL. EVEN WITHIN THE REALM OF THIS BOOK WHERE WE ARE TALKING ONLY ABOUT TROUT AND TROUT STREAMS, ALL WATERS ARE NOT CREATED EQUAL. SOME WATERS ARE BETTER THAN OTHERS, SOME ARE JUST DIFFERENT.

EDDY

CHUTE

EDDY

UNDERCUT BANK

SHALLOWS

RIFFLE

OVERHANGING TREES

TRIBUTARY

IN ADDITION TO THE DIFFERENT KINDS OF TROUT STREAMS, THERE ARE DIFFERENT PARTS OF EACH STREAM, AS WELL AS A VERITABLE PLETHORA OF CONSTANT OR CHANGING STREAM CHARACTERISTICS.

LEDGE

SUBMERGED LOG

EDDY

HEAD OF POOL

THE MOST ACCOMPLISHED FISHERS CAN WALK A NEW STRETCH OF STREAM AND MAKE A VERY EDUCATED GUESS WHERE THE FISH WILL BE.

Freestone

FREESTONE STREAMS ARE CHARACTERIZED BY A BOTTOM OF COARSE GRAVEL, COBBLE AND BOULDERS. MOST OFTEN, BUT NOT ALWAYS, WATER LEVELS ARE DEPENDENT ON RUNOFF AND FEEDER STREAMS. HIGH GRADIENT FREESTONE STREAMS MAY BE HEAVILY PUNCTUATED WITH LOTS OF POCKET WATER, PERFECT FOR HIDING TROUT. FREESTONE STREAMS ARE NOT ALWAYS FAST, SOMETIMES THEY ARE WIDE AND SLOW FLOWING.

Limestone

LIMESTONE STREAMS MAY OFTEN NOT FLOW AS FAST AS THE FASTEST FREESTONE STREAMS, BUT THEY CAN BE PLENTY FAST ENOUGH. MANY LIMESTONE STREAMS ARE SPRING FED AND MARKED BY A CLASSIC RIFFLE-RUN-POOL-FLAT MAKE-UP. WHILE GRAVEL, COBBLE AND BOULDERS WILL BE PRESENT, YOU WILL ALSO DISCOVER LIMESTONE BEDROCK STREAM FLOORS.

Tailwaters

TAILWATERS ARE THE STREAMS BELOW LARGE DAMS. SOME TAILWATERS ARE FAMOUS FOR THEIR TROPHY SIZE TROUT. AT THEIR BEST, TAILWATERS MAINTAIN CONSISTENTLY COOL TEMPERATURES AND WATER LEVELS WITHIN A REASONABLE RANGE. AT THEIR WORST, TAILWATERS ARE THE POOREST POSSIBLE SUBSTITUTE FOR A NATURAL ENVIRONMENT.

Spring Creeks

SPRING CREEKS ARE, AS THEIR NAME IMPLIES, FED BY GROUNDWATER SPRINGS. THERE ARE BOTH FREESTONE AND LIMESTONE SPRING CREEKS. SPRING CREEKS HOLD A SPECIAL PLACE IN THE HEARTS OF TROUT ANGLERS.

Holding Lies

HOLDING LIES ARE PLACES WHERE TROUT CAN REST FROM PREDATORS IN RELATIVE SAFETY. IN THE BEST HOLDING LIE, TROUT ARE DIFFICULT TO SEE, AND THEY HAVE GOOD ESCAPE ROUTES. DEEP, DARK WATER, UNDERCUT BANKS AND WEED BEDS ARE ALL EXAMPLES OF HOLDING LIES.

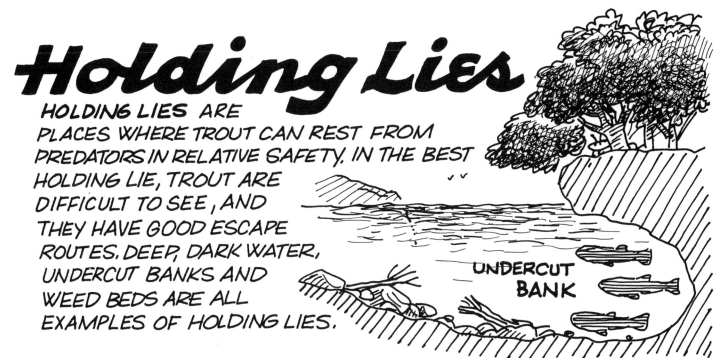

UNDERCUT BANK

Feeding Lies

FEEDING LIES ARE THE EATERIES OF THE TROUT'S WORLD. FEEDING LIES ARE THE PLACES IN A STREAM WHERE TROUT RECEIVE THEIR NOURISHMENT. FEEDING LIES MAY BE ANYPLACE WHERE A LOT OF FOOD IS AVAILABLE NATURALLY OR WHERE THE STREAM "DELIVERS" FOOD, SUCH AS EDDIES OR CURRENT SEAMS.

EDDY

EDDY

Prime Lies

PRIME LIES PROVIDE THE BEST OF ALL WORLDS. PRIME LIES OFFER GOOD COVER AND AN ABUNDANT FOOD SUPPLY ALL IN ONE PLACE. A DEEP UNDERCUT WHERE FAST WATER COMES AROUND A BEND IN THE STREAM WOULD BE JUST ONE EXAMPLE OF A PRIME LIE.

Riffles

RIFFLES ARE USUALLY FAIRLY SHALLOW & HAVE THE FASTEST WATER IN THE STREAM. THEY ARE GREAT FOR MORNING & EVENING FISHING IN PARTICULAR, BUT THEY ARE DEPENDABLE FOOD DELIVERY SYSTEMS 24 HOURS A DAY.

Runs

RUNS HOLD DEEPER WATER AND HAVE A SLOWER CURRENT THAN RIFFLES. THEY OFTEN MAKE VERY GOOD HIDING PLACES FOR TROUT. TRY FISHING BOTH THE HEAD AND THE MOUTH OF A RUN, AS WELL AS ITS EDGES.

Pools

POOLS, WITH THEIR DEEP, SLOW-MOVING WATER, ARE ALWAYS A FAVORITE SPOT FOR SOME OF THE BIGGEST TROUT IN THE STREAM. IF YOUR SKILLS ARE UP TO IT, POOLS CAN BE A PRODUCTIVE PLACE FOR CASTING BIG FLIES. OFTEN YOU WILL SEE THE TROUT HOLDING IN POOLS. BUT REMEMBER, IF YOU HAVE SEEN THEM, THEY HAVE PROBABLY ALREADY SEEN YOU.

Flats

FLATS ARE THE KIND OF PLACE WHERE YOU CAN'T FIND A TROUT AT MIDDAY, BUT WHICH CAN COME ALIVE WITH FISH AT NIGHT. THE USUALLY SLOW, USUALLY SHALLOW FLATS PROVIDE LITTLE COVER, SO THE TROUT STAY AWAY UNTIL HIDDEN BY THE DARKNESS OF NIGHT.

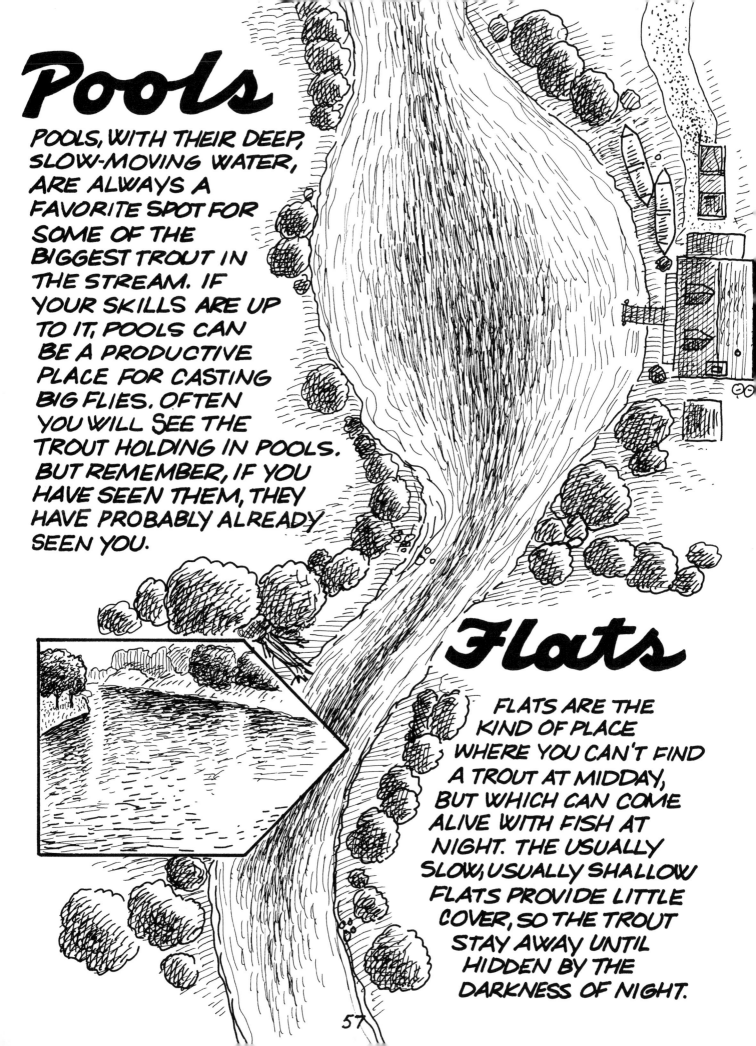

Eddies

EDDIES OCCUR BOTH DOWNSTREAM AND UPSTREAM OF OBSTRUCTIONS SUCH AS BOULDERS. THEIR SLOWLY FALLING CURRENT PROVIDES RELIEF FROM FASTER SURROUNDING WATERS, WHILE AT THE SAME TIME SERVING AS AN EXCELLENT FOOD DELIVERY SYSTEM.

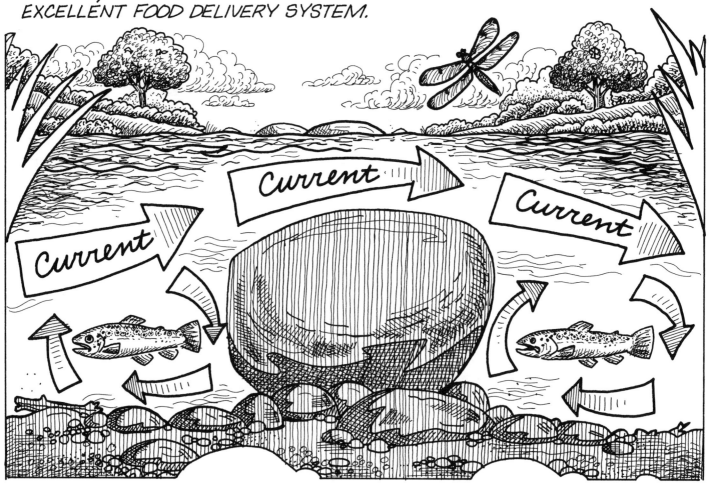

FLIES MUST BE PRESENTED **CAREFULLY.** WHEN THEY ARE, THE REWARD CAN BE A STRIKE SUDDEN OR SUBTLE, DEPENDING AT WHAT LEVEL THE FISH ARE FEEDING. ANGLERS WHO FISH ONLY DOWNSTREAM EDDIES ARE MISSING A LOT OF ACTION!

Undercut Banks

UNDERCUT BANKS MIGHT BE THE BEST COVER OF ALL. SOME UNDERCUTS ARE SO DEEP THAT THE TROUT ARE UNREACHABLE. IF THE CURRENT IS STILL NEXT TO THE BANK OR SWIRLS INTO IT, IT IS PROBABLY UNDERCUT. IF THE CURRENT IS FLOWING TIGHT TO THE BANK, THE BANK PROBABLY ISN'T UNDERCUT.

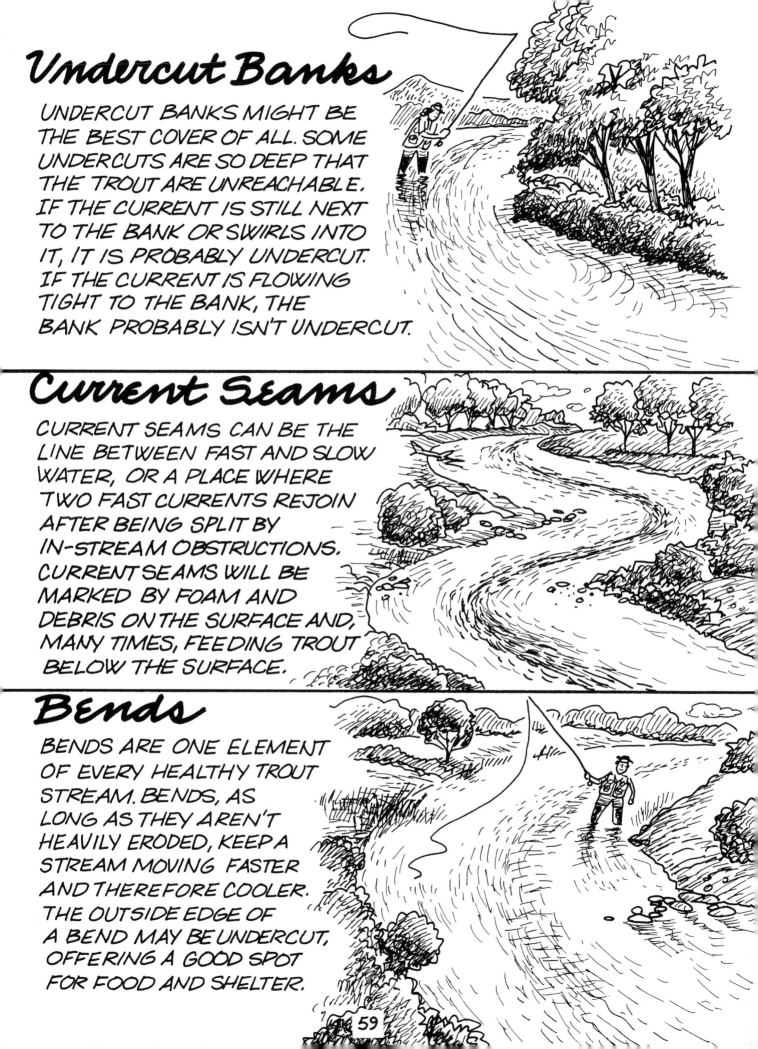

Current Seams

CURRENT SEAMS CAN BE THE LINE BETWEEN FAST AND SLOW WATER, OR A PLACE WHERE TWO FAST CURRENTS REJOIN AFTER BEING SPLIT BY IN-STREAM OBSTRUCTIONS. CURRENT SEAMS WILL BE MARKED BY FOAM AND DEBRIS ON THE SURFACE AND, MANY TIMES, FEEDING TROUT BELOW THE SURFACE.

Bends

BENDS ARE ONE ELEMENT OF EVERY HEALTHY TROUT STREAM. BENDS, AS LONG AS THEY AREN'T HEAVILY ERODED, KEEP A STREAM MOVING FASTER AND THEREFORE COOLER. THE OUTSIDE EDGE OF A BEND MAY BE UNDERCUT, OFFERING A GOOD SPOT FOR FOOD AND SHELTER.

Plunge Pools

PLUNGE POOLS FORM AT THE BOTTOM OF FALLS. EVEN SMALL OR MANMADE FALLS WILL HAVE A PLUNGE POOL FORMED BY THE FORCE OF THE FALLING WATER. THE DEPTH OF THE PLUNGE POOL WILL BE DETERMINED BY THE HEIGHT OF THE FALLS. FISH WILL CONGREGATE IN THE CALM WATER BELOW THE TURBULENCE OF THE PLUNGE POOL'S SWIRLING UPPER PORTION.

Step Pools

FORM IN THE SHORT SPACES BETWEEN A SERIES OF DESCENDING LEDGES. WATER ACTION IN STEP POOLS IS LESS DRAMATIC THAN IN PLUNGE POOLS, BUT THEY MAKE FINE TROUT HABITAT, ESPECIALLY IF THERE HAPPEN TO BE A FEW VERY LARGE ROCKS OR BOULDERS IN THE VICINITY. YOU CAN SOMETIMES SEE THE TROUT HOLDING IN STEP POOLS.

Step pools make for beautiful and complex fishing.

Weedbeds

ARE IGNORED BY SOME FLY FISHERS BECAUSE LURING FISH UP OUT OF THEM IS SUCH STEALTHY & SKILLFUL BUSINESS. WEED BEDS MAY SEEM TOO THICK TO HOLD EVEN A SINGLE FISH & YET BE FULL OF THEM.

Bridges

ARE TRUE MASTERWORKS. THEY GIVE HUMANS AN EASIER ROUTE ACROSS STREAMS, AND THEY GIVE FISH A GREAT PLACE TO REST AND DINE.

UNDER BRIDGES EXPECT SOME FASTER WATER, SOME DEEPER WATER, AND A STEADY FOOD SUPPLY.

61

Stream Splits

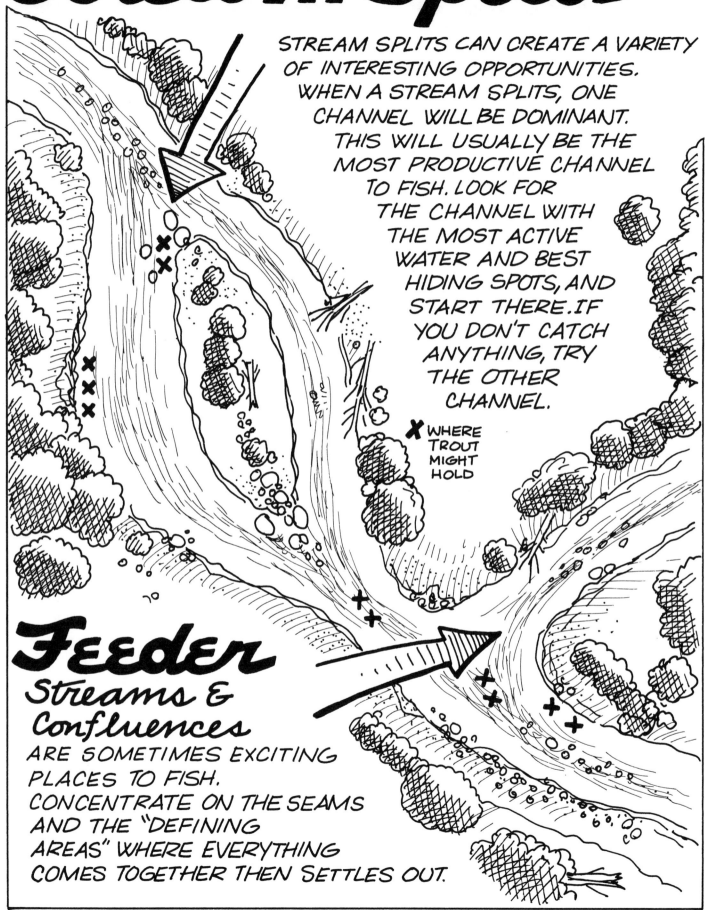

STREAM SPLITS CAN CREATE A VARIETY OF INTERESTING OPPORTUNITIES. WHEN A STREAM SPLITS, ONE CHANNEL WILL BE DOMINANT. THIS WILL USUALLY BE THE MOST PRODUCTIVE CHANNEL TO FISH. LOOK FOR THE CHANNEL WITH THE MOST ACTIVE WATER AND BEST HIDING SPOTS, AND START THERE. IF YOU DON'T CATCH ANYTHING, TRY THE OTHER CHANNEL.

✗ WHERE TROUT MIGHT HOLD

Feeder Streams & Confluences

ARE SOMETIMES EXCITING PLACES TO FISH. CONCENTRATE ON THE SEAMS AND THE "DEFINING AREAS" WHERE EVERYTHING COMES TOGETHER THEN SETTLES OUT.

FISHING DRY FLIES

DRY FLY FISHING MAY BE THE MOST PURE FORM OF FLY FISHING. EVERYTHING IS IN PLAIN SIGHT, THE FLY BOBS ALONG ON THE SURFACE OF THE WATER. WHEN A FISH STRIKES YOU SEE THE WHOLE SHOW.

THE PREFERRED DRY FLY CAST IS **UPSTREAM & ACROSS.** THIS APPROACH LETS YOU DRIFT YOUR FLY DOWN INTO THE TROUT'S WINDOW WITHOUT YOUR HAVING HAD TO CHANCE SPOOKING THE FISH BY CASTING DIRECTLY OVER ITS HEAD. ✱

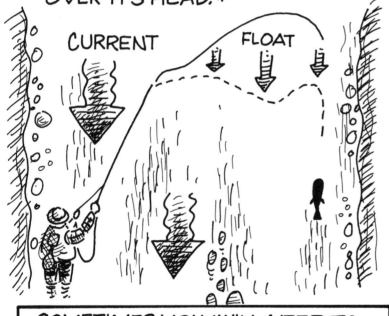

YOU WANT YOUR FLY TO DRIFT IN THE MOST NATURAL APPEARING WAY. USUALLY THIS MEANS A SIMPLE, DOWNSTREAM, **DRAG-FREE** FLOAT.

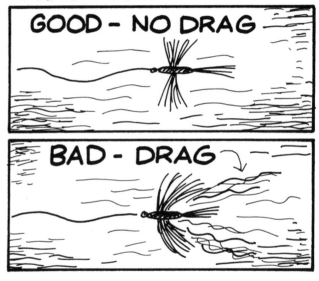

GOOD – NO DRAG

BAD – DRAG

SOMETIMES YOU WILL NEED TO IMPART ACTION TO YOUR FLY BY LIFTING THE ROD TIP AND **SKITTERING** OR **STRIPPING ERRATICALLY** TO IMITATE AN ESCAPING OR STRUGGLING BUG.

✱ CASTING DIRECTLY OVER THE TROUT'S HEAD SO THAT IT IS SPOOKED BY THE LINE IS CALLED **LINING** THE FISH.

FISHING NYMPHS

THE VAST MAJORITY OF A TROUT'S DIET COMES FROM UNDER WATER. SO YOU HAVE MANY MORE OPPORTUNITIES TO TAKE TROUT WITH **NYMPHS** AND THEIR LIKE THAN YOU DO WITH DRY FLIES. IT TAKES A LOT OF TIME AND PRACTICE TO BECOME AN ACCOMPLISHED NYMPH FISHER. (NOTE: YOU CAN CATCH FISH WHILE LEARNING.)

THERE ARE MANY TECHNIQUES AND TACTICS FOR FISHING THE NYMPH. TWO GOOD ONES TO BEGIN TO LEARN TO FISH THE NYMPH WITH ARE THE STANDARD **UP AND ACROSS WITH A DOWNSTREAM DRIFT** AND THE CLASSIC **LEISENRING LIFT.**

ON AN **UPSTREAM AND ACROSS** CAST, EITHER CAST WELL ABOVE THE FISH OR MEND LINE TO GIVE YOUR FLY TIME TO SINK BEFORE IT REACHES ITS TARGET.

CURRENT

LET THE FLY DRIFT DOWNSTREAM AND SWING ACROSS AT THE BOTTOM OF ITS DRIFT. AS THE FLY COMES ACROSS, TWITCH IT UPWARD. TROUT WILL OFTEN STRIKE JUST WHEN THE NYMPH SEEMS CERTAIN TO ESCAPE.

P.S. IF UPSTREAM AND ACROSS ISN'T PRODUCTIVE, TRY DOWNSTREAM AND ACROSS WITH A WIGGLE CAST.

THE LEISENRING LIFT

Before his death in 1951, James Leisenring developed or improved a number of fly patterns that are still used today. However, he is best known for the nymphing technique that carries his name, the LEISENRING LIFT.

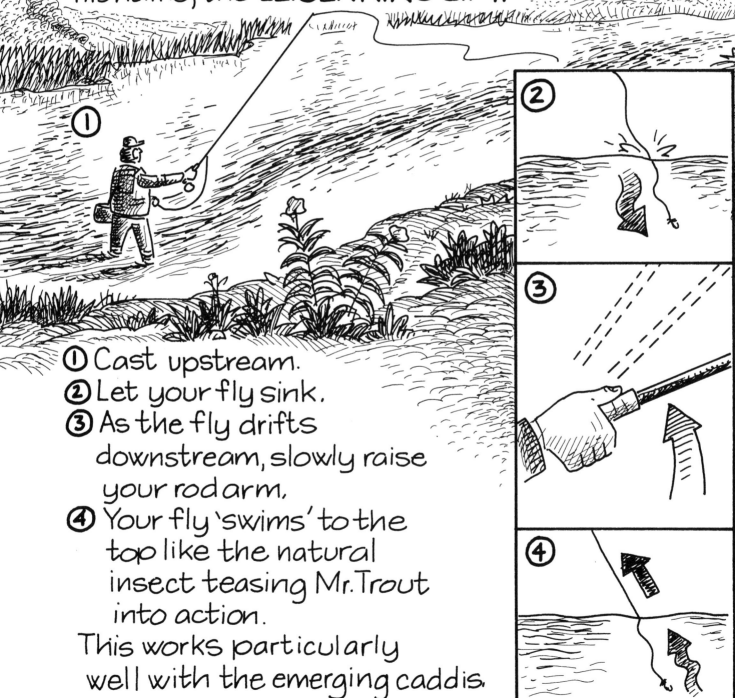

① Cast upstream.
② Let your fly sink.
③ As the fly drifts downstream, slowly raise your rod arm.
④ Your fly 'swims' to the top like the natural insect teasing Mr. Trout into action.

This works particularly well with the emerging caddis.

FISHING STREAMERS

Anglers are well advised to make **STREAMERS** a part of their arsenal, but not to be too hard on themselves during the learning process.

AS YOU ARE LEARNING TO FISH STREAMERS, WEIGHT THEM DOWN SLIGHTLY WITH A SMALL SPLIT SHOT OR BEAD HEAD AS YOU WOULD A NYMPH. (LATER YOU MAY WANT TO TRY FISHING STREAMERS WITH A SINK TIP LINE.)

THERE ARE SEVERAL POPULAR STREAMER TACTICS. PROBABLY THE MOST POPULAR AND ONE OF THE MOST PRODUCTIVE IS AN **ACROSS STREAM CAST** FOLLOWED BY A **VARIED RETRIEVE** AS THE FLY SWINGS DOWNSTREAM.

CURRENT

AN **ERRATIC RETRIEVE** SUGGESTS AN EASILY – BUT NOT TOO EASILY – CAPTURED MEAL. AS YOUR STREAMER COMPLETES ITS DOWNSTREAM SWING, RETRIEVE IT WITH A VARIETY OF RHYTHMS UNTIL YOU FIND ONE (OR MORE) THAT THE FISH LIKE.

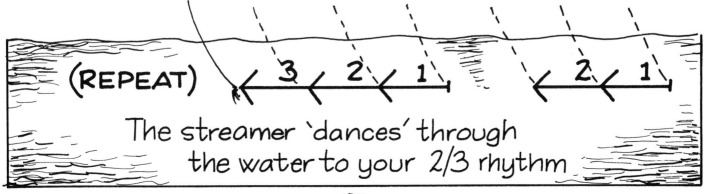

(REPEAT)   3   2   1   2   1

The streamer 'dances' through the water to your 2/3 rhythm

FISHING

TERRESTRIALS START OUT AS DRY FLIES. FISHED PROPERLY THEY MAY SOMETIMES BECOME WET FLIES.

For the most part, a terrestrial is fished much as a dry fly, even when it slips beneath the surface.

JUST KEEP IN MIND THAT REAL TERRESTRIALS USUALLY COME TO BE IN THE WATER BY VIRTUE OF HAVING FALLEN OFF STREAMSIDE VEGETATION. SO, CAST YOUR IMITATION TO THE EDGES OR CURRENT SEAMS WHERE THE NATURALS ARE MOST LIKELY TO BE.

DON'T WORRY WHEN YOUR TERRESTRIAL SWIRLS BELOW THE SURFACE; THE SAME THING HAPPENS TO THE NATURALS. SOMETIMES A FISH WON'T TAKE THE BUG UNTIL AFTER IT'S SUCKED UNDER.

STOP AT THE SHOP

ALWAYS STOP AT THE LOCAL FLY SHOP TO FIND OUT WHAT'S HAPPENING ON THE STREAM. WHAT BUGS ARE ACTIVE? WHAT ARE WATER CONDITIONS LIKE?

AND DON'T LEAVE UNTIL YOU'VE ASKED IF ANY PARTICULAR PRESENTATION HAS BEEN HOT. SOMETIMES IT'S NOT THE BUG AT ALL, BUT HOW YOU THROW AND RETRIEVE IT.

SIZE · SHAPE · COLOR

IMITATE THE FLIES YOU SEE IN THE WAY THEY LOOK & THE WAY THEY ACT IN THE WATER. WHEN IN DOUBT, OR WHEN YOUR FLY BOX FAILS TO YIELD UP JUST THE RIGHT FLY, REMEMBER THE **SIZE-SHAPE-COLOR** RULE:

SIZE · WHEN IN DOUBT, OPT FOR THE SMALLER FLY.

SHAPE · TRY TO DETERMINE THE GENERAL TYPE OF FLY IN THE WATER, ON THE WATER OR IN THE AIR & MAKE YOUR BEST GUESS.

COLOR · WHEN IN DOUBT, OPT FOR THE DARKER FLY.

NOTE:
KEEP A SMALL NET OR SEINE IN YOUR VEST, AND YOU WILL ALWAYS HAVE ONE HANDY.

USE THE SEINE TO FIND THE INSECT SPECIES THAT OCCUR IN THE SURFACE FILM.

KEEP YOUR DRIES DRY

USE ANY OF THE COMMERCIALLY AVAILABLE FLOATANTS TO KEEP YOUR DRY FLIES DRY. SOMETIMES FALSE CASTING ALONE WON'T DO THE TRICK. APPLY FLOATANT AS OFTEN AS NECESSARY, BUT NOT TOO OFTEN.

USE A DESICCANT POWDER TO REMOVE WATER OR FISH SLIME AFTER CATCHING A FISH.

NYMPHS DON'T FLOAT

SOME NYMPHS ARE TIED WITH LEAD OR LEAD SUBSTITUTES TO GET THEM DOWN FAST. THERE ARE ALSO DRESSINGS AVAILABLE TO HELP YOUR NYMPHS SINK. SPLIT SHOT IS AN OLD STANDARD THAT MAY NEVER BE REPLACED.

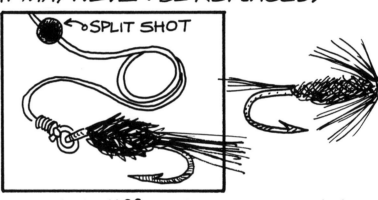

SPLIT SHOT

BEAD HEAD

If you want to try a little bit different approach, slide a bead onto your tippet before you tie on your fly. When you cast, the bead will slide down to the eye of the hook giving you an instant bead head <u>and</u> a nymph that sinks. (Yes, of course, the same trick works with streamers.)

SHARP HOOKS CATCH FISH

It's a good practice to sharpen all hooks before fishing with them. And keep them sharp. (Note: hooks with the barbs pinched down will penetrate the trout's lip with ease.)

CHECK YOUR KNOTS!

A weak or loose knot will not hold fish. Check your knots

every time you catch a fish or get hung up.

What the Trout Senses

THE ORIGINAL FISHEYE LENS

DORSAL FIN

ADIPOSE FIN

CHEEK

SMALL BRAIN (COMMONLY USED TO FOOL FLY FISHERS)

LATERAL LINE

GILL COVER

PELVIC FIN

TOOTHY SHARP TONGUED MOUTH

PECTORAL FIN

ANAL FIN

CAUDAL FIN

TROUT USE THEIR SENSE OF **SMELL** TO LOCATE FOOD, TO WARN OF AN ENEMY'S APPROACH AND TO FIND THEIR WAY HOME.

MAYBE YOU COULD CALL IT **HEARING**, MAYBE NOT, BUT A TROUT DOES EMPLOY ITS **LATERAL LINE** TO SENSE, OR "HEAR", SOUND - LIKE VIBRATIONS THROUGH THE WATER. **BE QUIET!**

SIGHT

TO CATCH TROUT, YOU MUST TAKE INTO CONSIDERATION THE TROUT'S **CONE OF VISION**. UNLESS YOU'VE BEEN STUDYING THIS STUFF, YOU WOULD PROBABLY UNDERESTIMATE THE TROUT'S ABILITY TO SEE.

THE AREA ON THE SURFACE OF THE WATER THAT THE TROUT SEES THROUGH IS CALLED ITS **WINDOW**. THE WINDOW IS CIRCULAR. THE SIZE OF THE WINDOW IS DETERMINED BY THE TROUT'S DEPTH IN THE WATER. THE DEEPER THE FISH, THE MORE IT CAN SEE. AND, THANKS TO **REFRACTION** (BENT LIGHT RAYS) AT THE SURFACE, THE TROUT'S WINDOW EXPANDS IN ALL DIRECTIONS. **STAY LOW!**

REFRACTION ANOTHER 10° TO SURFACE

THE TROUT'S WINDOW 97°

BE QUIET!

JUST BECAUSE THEY DON'T HAVE EARS DOESN'T MEAN TROUT CAN'T HEAR. KEEP NOISE TO A MINIMUM. WHEN YOU WADE IN SLOW WATER, MOVE SLOW.

HIDE BEHIND STUFF...

IN ADDITION TO STAYING LOW AND BEING QUIET, YOU SHOULD ALSO TAKE ADVANTAGE OF STREAMSIDE AND MIDSTREAM ROCKS AND VEGETATION TO KEEP YOUR PRESENCE HIDDEN FROM WARY TROUT.

WHEN POSSIBLE, TRY TO STAY IN THE SHADOWS.

STAY LOW!

And we do mean LOW! If necessary crawl to the stream & cast from your knees. Some of those old-timers who talk about crawling on their bellies to get to their favorite stream aren't kidding.

SNEAK UPSTREAM

TROUT GENERALLY FEED FACING **UPSTREAM**, SO YOU STAND A BETTER CHANCE BY COMING UP FROM BEHIND AND FISHING UPSTREAM.

DON'T LINE 'EM

CAST AT AN ANGLE AND AHEAD OF FISH SO YOUR LINE DOESN'T FLY OVER THEIR HEADS WHERE THEY'LL SEE IT AND BE STARTLED.

THE CURRENT WILL 'DELIVER' THE FLY TO FEEDING TROUT

NO SHADOWS

IF YOU PUT YOURSELF BETWEEN THE SUN & THE FISH, CHANCES ARE YOUR SHADOW WILL SPOOK THE LATTER. FISH SO THAT YOUR SHADOW FALLS BEHIND YOU OR IS IN SOME OTHER WAY HIDDEN FROM YOUR PREY.

Night Fishing

Night fishing is an eerie world apart from all other fly fishing

Never fish an area at night that you haven't first scouted thoroughly during daylight.

FISHING AT NIGHT TAKES PRACTICE, SKILL AND **EXTREME CAUTION!**

There is the obvious problem created by little or no light. There is also the fact that a number of creatures are out at night foraging and hunting for food.

The reward for fishing at night can be huge trout that would never dream of coming out from cover during daylight hours.

HOW TO KNOW WHEN A FISH TAKES YOUR FLY

PART OF THE CHARM OF FISHING DRY FLIES IS THAT THEY ADD SO MUCH TO THE VISUAL APPRECIATION OF FISHING.

HEAD & TAIL RISE

SIP

SPLASH

WHEN A FISH TAKES A DRY FLY, IT'S PRETTY OBVIOUS. SOMETIMES THE TAKE WILL BE VIOLENT. OTHER TIMES, THE FISH WILL SIP IN THE FLY FROM JUST BELOW THE SURFACE. EITHER WAY, IT'S CLEAR WHAT HAS HAPPENED.

STREAMERS CAN'T USUALLY BE SEEN AS YOU FISH THEM, BUT THE STRIKE THEY INDUCE IS TYPICALLY DRAMATIC. THE LINE STRAIGHTENS. THE ROD BENDS AND PULSES.

HOW TO KNOW... cont'd

NYMPHS ARE TRICKY. WHEN A FISH TAKES A NYMPH, YOUR LINE MAY DART FORWARD OR HESITATE IN THE CURRENT FOR AN INSTANT, IT TAKES SOME TIME TO LEARN TO SEE WITH THE EYE OF THE SKILLED NYMPH FISHER.

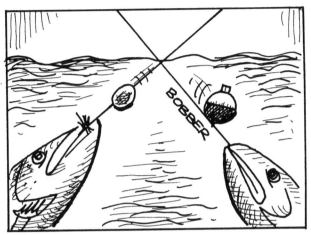

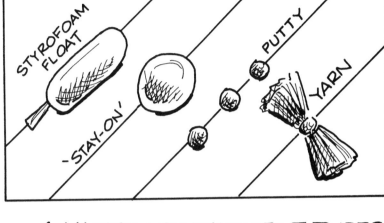

STRIKE INDICATORS ARE AN EXCELLENT VISUAL AID TO THE BEGINNING NYMDHER. CALL THEM WHAT YOU WILL, THEY WORK MUCH LIKE AN OLD FASHIONED BOBBER.

A VARIETY OF DIFFERENT TYPES OF STRIKE INDICATORS ARE AVAILABLE COMMERCIALLY, YOU CAN EVEN BUY STRIKE PUTTY THAT MOLDS ONTO YOUR LINE, OR, YOU CAN MAKE YOUR OWN STRIKE INDICATOR WITH A PIECE OF YARN.

ATTACH THE STRIKE INDICATOR AT A PLACE ON THE TIPPET OR LEADER THAT ALLOWS THE NYMPH TO FLOAT JUST ABOVE BOTTOM.

IF THE STRIKE INDICATOR DARTS FORWARD, PULLS UNDER THE SURFACE OR STALLS IN THE CURRENT, SET THE HOOK. CHANCES ARE FAIR A FISH HAS STRUCK!

The Strike!

When the fish STRIKES your fly, you must STRIKE quickly!

Timing is everything. Practice will bring the perfect timing that allows you to set the hook in the instant between the time the fish takes the fly into its mouth and then, finding it to be an imitation, spits it out.

YOUR STRIKE MUST BE SUDDEN, BUT NOT TOO HARD. TOO HARD A STRIKE IS LIKELY TO EITHER BREAK YOUR TIPPET OR WORSE, INJURE THE TROUT'S SOFT MOUTH.

To **set the hook,** lift your rod tip with a firm, steady pressure. At the same time maintain a grip on the line with your line hand to keep out slack.

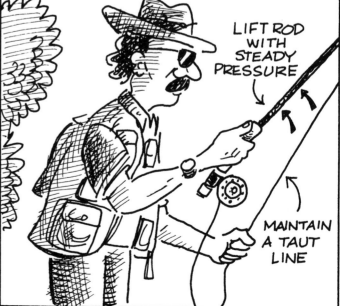

PLAYING THE FISH

When you finally hook your first trout on a fly, your next challenge is to land it!

Trout have soft mouths. You don't need to set the hook hard, just lift your rod tip with a firm, steady pressure.

Maintain a tight line at all times.

Play & land the fish as fast as possible. But when a fish runs, let him have his head while maintaining light tension on the line.

As often as not at first, you will bring in the fish by hand-stripping line rather than using the reel. Learn early, however, to get fish on the reel & play them from there.

CATCH & RELEASE

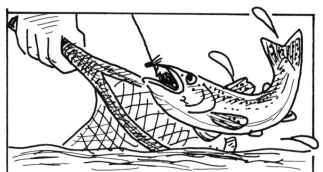

When you have a fish close in & tired, net it head first by dipping the net under & up quickly. Avoid playing fish to exhaustion. Try not to chase the fish with the net.

Never grab a wet fish with your hands dry. This may destroy the protective slime on the fish's body & limit its chances of survival when you release it.

Hold the fish across its back & head. Turn the fish belly up. To remove the fly, grasp the hook near the bottom of the bend with your forceps & pull out firmly.

No self-respecting fly fisher goes astream without a proper tool to aid in the release of captured fish. **Forceps** - little multi-purpose masterworks that they are - have been the tool of choice for years. Some fishers have, however, found more "modern" tools, such as the Ketchum Release (tm), to be the most effective in fish liberation.

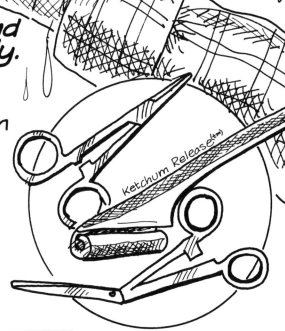

Ketchum Release (tm)

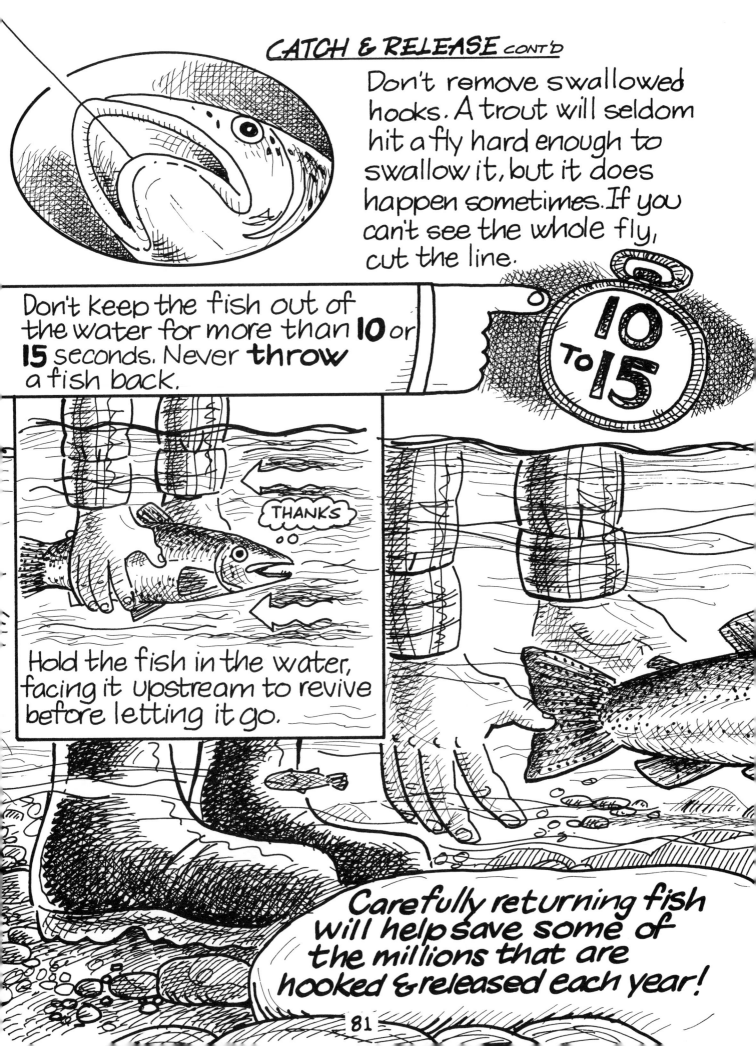

CATCH & RELEASE CONT'D

Don't remove swallowed hooks. A trout will seldom hit a fly hard enough to swallow it, but it does happen sometimes. If you can't see the whole fly, cut the line.

Don't keep the fish out of the water for more than **10** or **15** seconds. Never **throw** a fish back.

10 TO 15

THANKS

Hold the fish in the water, facing it upstream to revive before letting it go.

Carefully returning fish will help save some of the millions that are hooked & released each year!

WATCH YOUR STEP ON LAND

THERE ARE SOME HAZARDS THAT APPEAR EVERYWHERE IN THE LAND OF THE FREE AND THE HOME OF THE BRAVE. OTHERS OCCUR IN CERTAIN REGIONS ONLY. BE ALERT TO POTENTIAL HAZARDS AND EDUCATE YOURSELF ABOUT HAZARDS UNIQUE TO YOUR AREA.

POISONOUS PLANTS

Poison Ivy or Poison Oak

Stinging Nettle

← SHARP BRITTLE HAIRS

BUGS

THAT BITE, STING AND OTHERWISE CAUSE DISCOMFORT.

← BEES

TICKS
CHECK CLOTHING & BODY—
TO REMOVE COVER WITH OIL (MINERAL OR SALAD) AND REMOVE TICK WITH TWEEZERS BY TURNING COUNTERCLOCKWISE

SPIDERS

BROWN RECLUSE

BLACK WIDOW

RED ⊠ SHAPE ON UNDERSIDE

LOOK OUT

WATCH YOUR STEP ON LAND

(ALL RATTLESNAKES ARE POISONOUS!)

RATTLESNAKES CAN BE FASCINATING, BUT THEY ARE DEADLY. THE SAME GOES FOR TARANTULAS AND SCORPIONS.

BE CAREFUL NOT TO STARTLE ANIMALS WITH PARTICULARY OFFENSIVE PROTECTIVE RESPONSES. (SKUNKS AND PORCUPINES)

HOLES APPEAR WHERE YOU LEAST EXPECT THEM, WATCH YOUR STEP AND TEST THE GROUND AHEAD.

STEEP BANKS, WET BANKS, LEAF COVERED AND CLAY BANKS CAN ALL BE DANGEROUS. FELT SOLED BOOTS WILL HELP KEEP YOU ERECT IN THE WATER, BUT WILL SOMETIMES DROP YOU UNEXPECTEDLY ON LAND.

WALK! DON'T RUN

WATCH FOR SNAKES ON STREAM BANKS

IN THE WATER

WATCH YOUR STEP!

STEP LIGHTLY, WATCH WHERE YOU'RE GOING, BE CAREFUL.

Creeks and rivers are our friends, but like any wild thing, there are times when they act upon their nature and turn. **THEY DESERVE OUR RESPECT.**

SHUFFLE ALONG, TESTING AHEAD WITH ONE FOOT – OR BETTER YET WITH A STAFF – TO AVOID STUMBLING OVER SUBMERGED ROCKS, BRANCHES OR LOGS.

OLD BROOM STICKS & MOP HANDLES MAKE SUPERB WALKING STAFFS. USE A LONG PIECE OF RAWHIDE BOOT STRING TO MAKE A SHOULDER STRAP.

A STAFF WILL ALSO ALERT YOU TO THE DEPTH OF MUCK HOLES, SUCK HOLES AND DROP-OFFS.

WHEN CROSSING A FAST-MOVING STREAM, ANGLE DOWNSTREAM AND GO WITH THE CURRENT.

IN THE WATER

WATCH YOUR STEP!

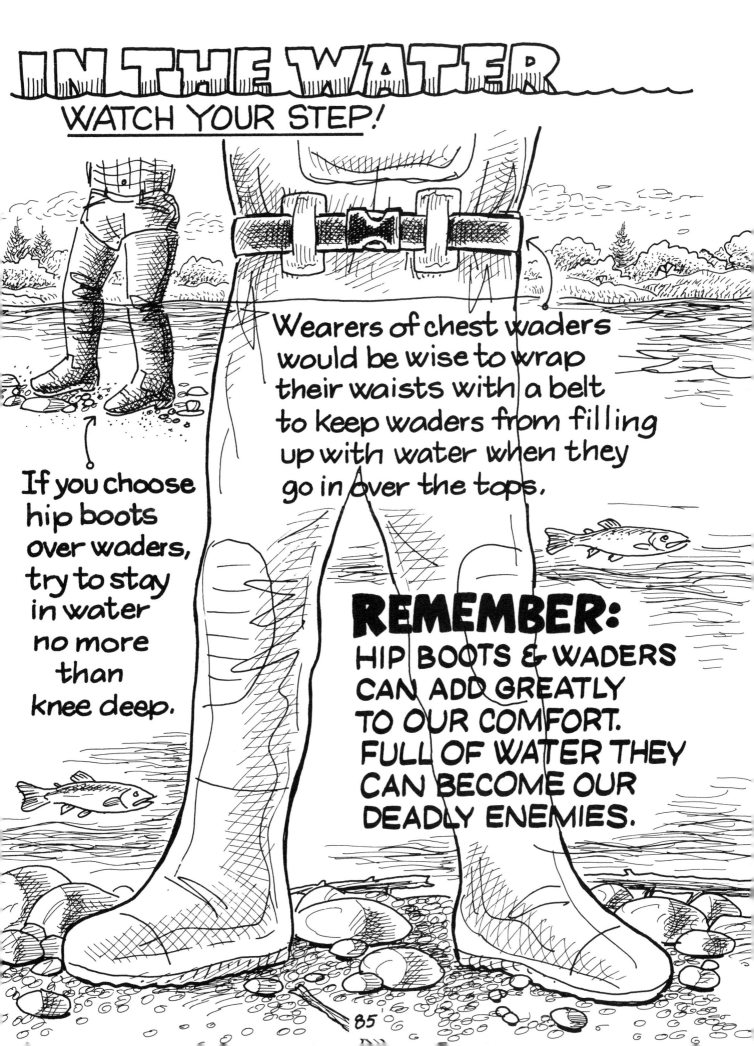

If you choose hip boots over waders, try to stay in water no more than knee deep.

Wearers of chest waders would be wise to wrap their waists with a belt to keep waders from filling up with water when they go in over the tops.

REMEMBER:
HIP BOOTS & WADERS CAN ADD GREATLY TO OUR COMFORT. FULL OF WATER THEY CAN BECOME OUR DEADLY ENEMIES.

IN THE WATER

WATCH YOUR STEP!

ALL UNDERWATER HAZARDS ARE NOT CREATED BY MOTHER NATURE

NO DUMPING

UNWARY WADERS ARE SOMETIMES FELLED BY STRANDS OF WIRE, DISCARDED TIRES AND OTHER MEMORIALS TO IGNORANCE AND STUPIDITY. (DON'T ADD TO THE PROBLEM: DISPOSE OF YOUR TRASH RESPONSIBLY & PICK UP LITTER YOU FIND ALONG YOUR WAY.)

CAUTION!

EVEN THE NARROWEST STREAMS ARE OCCASIONALLY PUNCTUATED BY UNCHARACTERISTICALLY DEEP HOLES, RUNS AND POOLS.

WADING CHAINS

FELT SOLES PREVENT SLIPPING ON SOME GREASE-SLICK SURFACES, BUT MANY FISHERS PREFER RUBBER SOLES. RUBBER CLEATS, STEEL STUDS AND SLIP-ON CHAINS CAN ALSO HELP KEEP YOU SURE-FOOTED.

RUBBER SOLE WITH CLEATS FITS OVER BOOTS

IN THE WATER

WATCH YOUR STEP!

IF YOU DO TAKE A DUNKING, **DON'T PANIC.** LAY BACK, POINT YOUR FEET DOWNSTREAM AND WAIT FOR THE WATER TO CARRY YOU TO A SHALLOW SPOT.

CURRENT

WADE WITH A FRIEND

MANY POTENTIAL PECCADILLOS OF THE WATERY KIND CAN BE AVOIDED COMPLETELY BY WADING WITH A PARTNER. AND, OF COURSE, WHEN THINGS DO GO WRONG, IT'S NICE TO HAVE A FRIEND TO PULL YOU OUT.

Weather Awareness

EXTREME WEATHER CONDITIONS ARE AS MUCH A DANGER IN THE WATER AS THEY ARE AT ANY OTHER TIME OR IN ANY OTHER LOCATION.

A COUPLE OF CONDITIONS ARE OF PARTICULAR IMPORTANCE TO ANGLERS:

SUN

WHEN YOU GO OUT TO SPEND THE DAY ON A TROUT STREAM, COVER ALL EXPOSED BODY PARTS WITH **SUNSCREEN.**

SUNBLOCK 50 SPF

Between the sun's direct rays & those that bounce up off the water, you can get a nasty burn before you know it.

LIGHTNING

IF THERE IS **LIGHTNING** ANYWHERE IN SIGHT OR IT LOOKS LIKE THERE COULD BE ANYTIME SOON, GET OUT OF THE WATER AND UNDER COVER.

MIKE'S DINER

FOOD

GO FISH

WATER AND GRAPHITE ARE TWO OF THE BEST CONDUCTORS OF ELECTRICITY THERE ARE — *DON'T BECOME A HUMAN LIGHTNING ROD!*

HOW TO REMOVE A HOOK
FROM YOUR FRIEND OR YOURSELF

IT'S AMAZING THE NUMBER OF PLACES ON A PERSON HOOKS MANAGE TO GET STUCK IN. ARMS, LEGS, EARS, NOSES, EYES: IT WOULD SEEM NO PART IS SAFE.

Hats and sunglasses, long sleeve shirts and long legged pants all help keep hooks from becoming imbedded in flesh. Bandannas are not only stylish, they also help necks and throats remain hook free.

WHEN A HOOK DOES FIND FLESH, YOU SHOULD HAVE SOME IDEA HOW TO REMOVE IT....

HAT

SUNGLASSES

BANDANNA

LONG SLEEVE SHIRT

WADERS OR OTHER LEG PROTECTION

EASY HOOK REMOVAL ✚

① IF THE HOOK IS STUCK JUST UNDER THE SKIN, CUT THE LEADER (WITHOUT PULLING ON IT.)

② THEN RUN A LINE (HEAVY LEADER OR FLY LINE) THROUGH THE HOOK BEND WITH ENOUGH LENGTH TO GET A GOOD GRIP ON THE ENDS.

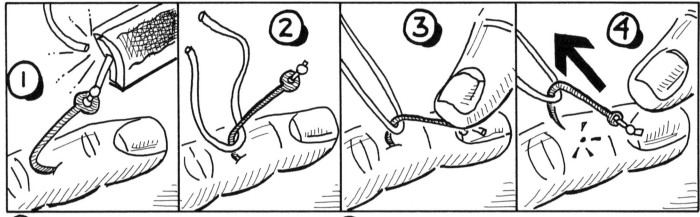

③ PUSH THE HOOK EYE DOWN AGAINST THE SKIN.

④ PULL THE HOOK OUT WITH A FIRM, FAST MOTION.

NOT-SO-EASY HOOK REMOVAL

YOU CAN SOMETIMES REMOVE HOOKS THAT HAVE PENETRATED TO THE POINT THAT THEY ARE BEGINNING TO POKE BACK OUT.

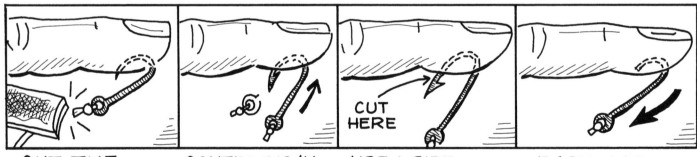

CUT HERE

CUT THE LEADER.

CONTINUING IN THE DIRECTION THE HOOK IS ALREADY HEADING, PUSH SO THAT THE BARB IS CLEAR OF THE SKIN.

USE A SIDE CUTTING PLIERS TO CUT OFF THE POINT & BARB.

BACK THE HOOK OUT THE SAME WAY IT WENT IN.

~~~CAUTION!~~~
DON'T REMOVE HOOKS FROM EYES, THE NECK, THROAT OR HEAD! GET TO A DOCTOR AS SOON AS POSSIBLE!

AFTERWARD: ONCE A HOOK IS REMOVED, RINSE THE INJURED AREA WITH ALCOHOL, PEROXIDE, LISTERINE OR GOOD WHISKEY. COVER WITH A STERILE PAD. CONSULT A DOCTOR WHEN YOU ARE ABLE.

THE TROUTS (& CHAR)

The streams of the United States hold many species of trout and char. Rainbows and steelhead, cutthroats, goldens and browns are all actual **trout**. Brook trout, bull trout and Dolly Vardens belong to the **char** family.

RAINBOW TROUT
SALMO GAIRDNERI GAIRDNERI

PINK

Many small black spots on body. Square tail with many spots in radiating rows. Pink horizontal stripe along lateral line and pink gill cover. White mouth and gums.

STEELHEAD
ONCORHYNCHUS GAIRDNERI

Spots all over tail and above lateral line. Silver body. May have very light pink lateral line and gill cover. White mouth.

YELLOWSTONE CUTTHROAT
ONCORHYNCHUS CLARKI BOUVIERI

Species name from William Clark who explored their western range with Meriwether Lewis. All cutthroats have a pair of red or orange slashes on the throat. Black spots on tail and body, with more spots to rear.

WESTSLOPE CUTTHROAT
ONCORHYNCHUS CLARKI LEWISI

More spots to rear of body than Yellowstone cutthroat and fewer, if any, spots on lower front half of body. As with other cutthroats, varying degrees of red/orange/pink on gill covers and along lateral line.

COASTAL CUTTHROAT
ONCORHYNCHUS CLARKI CLARKI

Silver body. Black spots over most of body. Lighter slash marks than other cutthroats.

GOLDEN TROUT
ONCORHYNCHUS MYKISS

PINK

Golden along flanks. Red along lateral line and on gill covers. White edge tips on dorsal, pelvic and anal fins. Dark ovals along sides.

BROWN TROUT
SALMO TRUTTA

Imported to the U.S. from Germany and elsewhere. Large black, blue and/or red spots on brownish body with yellow belly. Square tail with few if any spots.

BROOK TROUT
SALVELINUS FONTINALIS

Also known as speckled trout or specks. Irregular wormlike markings on back and dorsal fin. Square tail. Reddish spots with blue halos. Pinkish lower fins edged in white.

BULL TROUT
SALVELINUS CONFULLENTUS

Pink and/or white spots with green body. White leading edge on lower fin.

DOLLY VARDEN
SALVELINUS MALMA

Green to silver body. Pink and/or red spots on most of body. White leading edge on lower fins.

THE MOST COMMON TROUTS

RAINBOW

BROWN

WESTSLOPE CUTTHROAT

BROOK

CONSERVATION

TWO GROUPS THAT WORK

TAKE AN ACTIVE PART IN THE CONSERVATION OF OUR COLD WATER FISHERIES! WE RECOMMEND 2 ORGANIZATIONS THAT ALLOW YOU TO MAKE A DIFFERENCE. BOTH HAVE LOCAL CHAPTERS WITH ONGOING PROJECTS SO YOU CAN MAKE A MEANINGFUL CONTRIBUTION IN YOUR OWN AREA.

TROUT UNLIMITED

was founded in Grayling, Michigan in 1959. Today TU is a huge organization committed to conserving, protecting & restoring America's wild trout & salmon. A great deal of TU's good works are carried out on a grass roots level. TU is one of the most truly active & effective environmental groups we have ever seen. TU expects and gets much more from its members than money. For info write: **TROUT UNLIMITED**
1500 WILSON BOULEVARD
SUITE 310
ARLINGTON, VA 22209

THE FEDERATION OF FLY FISHERS

founded in 1965, has a ways to go before it equals Trout Unlimited in total memberships, but it is a large & growing organization. The FFF's mission is no small one either. Many of FFF's programs & projects cover similar ground to TU's, but one area where the FFF is unique is that its area of concern extends to "all fish, all waters." For info write: **FEDERATION OF FLY FISHERS**
P.O. BOX 1595
BOZEMAN, MT 59771

END NOTES

And now it is time for you to take the words and pictures you have found in this book and turn them into your own reality

Go forth. Find a stream you can fish often, and learn it. This is your home water. Talk to others who fish your stream, especially the old guys who have been fishing it for years. If your stream has been written about, read those words, and digest them.

Study your home water. Learn all you can. This is the foundation of all the fly fishing you will do from here on out.